Track of the Kodiak

Track of the Kodiak

by: Marvin H. Clark, Jr.

*Great Northwest Publishing
and Distributing Company
Anchorage, Alaska
1984*

Dedicated to
My Alaskan Partners,
my loving wife Olga, who joined me by faith from 12,000 miles,
and my children,
Alaina, Alissa, Rachel and Jonathan
who fill my life
with all things good and wonderful

INTRODUCTION

No sooner did I complete the Pinnell and Talifson story, than I began realizing that my work on Kodiak was incomplete. That book contained the story of two guides. Another book was necessary to tell the story of the Brown Bear and the land. This is what I have attempted to do in **Track of the Kodiak**.

I traveled to Kodiak in the late 1970's and spent almost a month backpacking across the island, photographing, and refreshing my memory of what I had learned as an assistant guide. Additional research on Kodiak Island's ancient past was more recently accomplished. I hope that what has been prepared will be appreciated by all those who desire a more complete knowledge of Brown Bears and the land they inhabit. This has been my purpose; if I am successful in this endeavor, then I will be happy indeed.

Happy Hunting
the author

ACKNOWLEDGMENTS

I am grateful to my wife, who tolerated my many hours of seclusion while writing this book. I am also grateful to Professor Charles Keim, whose prior instruction at University of Alaska enabled me to acquire the necessary abilities. Finally, I am grateful to my parents, for permitting my original Alaskan explorations to occur so many years ago.

CONTENTS

Chapter I   The original trek; the author lands at Larsen's Bay   13
              and backpacks to Karluk Lake where he encounters
              bears and hunters.

Chapter II   Arrival at Bill Pinnell's Karluk Lake camp; hard-   21
              hunting with the master guide.

Chapter III   Return to Olga Bay; the Pinnell and Talifson story.   31

Chapter IV   Caring for hides with Morris Talifson.   59

Chapter V   Trek to Red Lake; through the world's largest bear   67
              trail; Kodiak's geographical and geological develop-
              ment considered.

Chapter VI   Weathered in at Red Lake; ancient Koniag history   73
              and culture.

Chapter VII   Russian America; early development under United   101
              States rule.

Chapter VIII Kodiak Blacktail deer; Reindeer; other species.   109

Chapter IX   Brown Bear life history; infanticide.   117

Chapter X   Trek to the sea; Brown Bear seasonal movement;   127
              denning habits.

Chapter XI   The danger factor considered; charging Brown   151
              Bears.

Chapter XII   Outfitting hunting camps.   163

Chapter XIII Trek to the head of Olga Bay; cabin politics and   175
              changing times.

Chapter XIV   Return to Cannery Cove; taxidermists and tanners;   197
              the skin scam.

Chapter XV   A parting shot; Pinnell and Talifson hunting   215
              methods explained.

CHAPTER I

Clouds of mist were falling in great sheets across the green and rust colored tundra as I sat resting after an arduous four-hour trek from Larsen Bay, on Kodiak Island's west side, to the top of the portage overlooking Karluk River Flats. The Kodiak Western Airways mail plane, an amphibious Grumman "Goose," had landed me at the mouth of Larsen's Bay shortly before noon. The early spring sun was shining brightly when I began walking, but now the sky was overcast. Because of the mist, I could barely distinguish the distant general vicinity of a U.S. Fish and Wildlife public-use cabin on the Karluk River where I planned to stay the night. A flock of ducks, seemingly unaffected by the dampness, flew overhead as I rested the frame of my 100-pound packboard against a large tussock. Water dripped from my raincoat, and I bemoaned the four miles separating me from shelter.

I was destined for Olga Bay, more than 50 miles away. To get there, I would travel through the interior of Kodiak's south end where the only roads are trails built by bears. I carried the usual pack outfit: tent, sleeping bag, food, gas stove, and fuel. I also toted a tripod, cameras, and a full assortment of lenses. The .375 H&H Magnum I packed added to this load; but on Kodiak Island, a good rifle is not a luxury, it's a necessity for protection against unexpected encounters with the world's largest bear: the Kodiak Brown Bear.

During the next four weeks I wanted to explore Brown Bear country and visit two of Alaska's most knowledgeable bear men, Bill Pinnell and Morris Talifson. I had been employed as a packer and assistant guide by these two famous guides during the Brown Bear hunting seasons of two years in the early 1970's, and spent most of the intervening months trapping and hunting throughout much of their territory. I later retained close ties to Brown Bear country by accepting summer work with a fishery company on Kodiak during my college years, and made several other trips into the island's wilderness. Now I was returning for yet another stint in bear country. The spring hunts still were taking place, and I hoped to arrive at the Pinnell and Talifson (P&T) camp at Karluk Lake before the outfit finished and returned to Olga Bay. That meant walking at least 35 miles, over rugged terrain, fully loaded, in just three days.

Finally resigning myself to the fact that landcruising on Kodiak Island is more work than fun, I contented myself for the moment to continue enjoying the damp comfort of my soft spot on a tussock.

Scanning the horizon with my binoculars, I beheld more than 200 square miles of open country — all of it bear country. The Karluk River was but a mere thread in the flats, flowing past the Sturgeon Mountains and out to sea. Acres of silver lichens and tundra moss laced with smaller patches of dead rye grass from the previous summer and arctic red willow covered the land. Hundreds of well-worn bear trails extended in literally every direction throughout the flats, creating a griddled appearance on the land. This sight reminded me of the many miles I had packed on such trails when guiding for P&T.

Suddenly, I became acutely aware that I was not alone. Indeed, on one of those trails less than 800 yards from where I sat, a large, dark object was slowly treading across the tundra.

"Bear!" I started with surprise.

The beast was moving through willows toward a large pond that lay some distance from where my trail was joined by several others. A southeast wind prevented the animal from getting my scent, and I wondered if it would turn toward me when it got to my trail. The beast was a good nine-footer, and a reassuring nudge at the stock of my .375 H&H Magnum gave me the confidence I needed. Several resident ducks exploded from the pond when they saw the creature, and the bruin observed their departure, perhaps a bit wistfully, having lost a good meal.

Then, on an opposing point less than 600 yards beyond the beast, I spotted two more, somewhat smaller objects. These were not bears but were distinctly human. I spotted them when one apparently stood up to remove a jacket from beneath his rain gear. A closer examination with my binoculars revealed that they both had rifles. Bear hunters!

My instincts as a former guide told me they had been scanning nearby slopes with high-powered glasses and had just spotted the bear that they were about to stalk. The hunter appeared to be removing excess garments to prevent overheating during the assault. I wondered if they could see me watching them. The unknowing Brown passed the portage trail without turning and continued toward the pond.

I could see that the animal was a real spring beauty and would make a fine trophy. An "unrubbed" spring bear hide often has the heaviest coat of fur obtainable, although November hides are quite heavy, too. The hunter fortunate enough to obtain such a skin has a beautiful prize. However, a *very* large percentage, up to 50 percent, of spring-season Kodiaks are rubbed — many quite badly. During the fall hunting season, only about nine percent of the bruins have rubs, and rarely is a fall hide rubbed badly. In the spring the "rubbed" fur may be rubbed or broken off almost next to the skin itself, leaving a large mat of stubby hair. During the fall, however, only the tips of guard hair may be broken, and these "rubs" may be barely noticeable. In any event, the bruin I observed apparently still possessed a fine coat, and the hunters probably were elated that they had found such a fine specimen.

The Brown had reached the pond and was gingerly pawing at some edible roots as the hunters began coming off the knoll. Seemingly, they would have little trouble stalking the beast. Once in the flats, however, the situation changed dramatically, because the hunters suddenly were standing level with the bear. Thick willows separated the adversaries, and the hunters no longer could see the animal constantly. The men apparently realized this as they entered the flats. They walked ever more cautiously as they advanced, and scoured the bush ahead of themselves with binoculars. When the hunters were less than 50 yards from the creature, which now was resting on its hind end, there still were willows between them and the bear. But I could see that an opening in the brush soon would present itself. I know the excitement that they must have felt and watched the two for what seemed an eternity as they moved ever closer to the Brown.

Then, as often occurs just when a hunter believes he is about to down a prize, the wind shifted 180 degrees. I felt a chill on the right side of my face as a northwest wind rushed past. Up came the bear! The beast, alerted by human scent, whipped around in an instant. It stood on all fours, facing the intruders from behind the willows with its nose lifted skyward. Although the men could not yet see the bear, they must have known that it probably was aware of their presence by now. Finally, the behemoth lifted itself onto its hind feet, high above the willows. I could almost feel the adrenalin pumping through those hunters' veins as the prize came into sight. But before either of them could fire, the beast lowered itself and quickly bolted away toward safety.

I watched the Kodiak flee from the hunters. It ran through willows and across the tundra, looking back periodically to see if it was being pursued. The hunters seemed confounded as they approached the spot where the Brown had stood. The bear was gone from sight; only its tracks remained in the rain-dampened tundra moss.

A deep chill passed over me as I witnessed the end of the excitement, and I once again longed to rest comfortably out of the weather. So, wedging myself between my packboard and the earth, I struggled to my feet and started down the trail. But I walked noticeably slower than the two hunters now were walking, without the weight of their hoped-for bear hide. I still had several miles to walk before reaching the river.

A low, steady column of smoke curled from the cabin smoke stack when I approached Karluk River. The rain had ceased, and gusts of wind whipped the smoke around in a circular motion before lifting it skyward. Light flickered from one of the cabin windows, and I saw a lone, tall figure packing water pails from the river. About 100 yards upstream stood another cabin that was older and obviously vacant. I mused that only one structure was identified on my map.

Evidently, the hunters I watched earlier were staying in the lower cabin. Moving closer, I saw that the man packing water appeared to be the same one who had removed his jacket before making the

16

stalk. He was an older man, with a lean and weathered look. When he saw me approaching on the trail, he set down his pails and leaned hard toward me as if sizing me up in the dim evening light. I called out a greeting.

"Hello!"

He didn't acknowledge my greeting but entered the cabin and closed the door. I stared in disbelief. Presently a younger man appeared, and seeing me, he stepped out of the door.

"Hello," I called again.

"Who are you?" he asked.

After explaining that I was packing cross-country to the P&T camp on Olga Bay, I told him that I had observed their attempted stalk earlier in the day. He seemed unimpressed with my story, and stared off toward the distant mountains to the west; then he pulled a pair of binoculars from his coat pocket and began scanning with them.

'We've seen a lot of bears this spring," he muttered.

"Where are you from?" I enquired.

"Over on the mainland."

Suddenly the older hunter reappeared in the cabin door. He was dressed in heavy woolens and wore "deck" shoes which are commonly worn by commercial fishermen around Alaska canneries.

"How long are you going to be around here?" he asked.

"Til morning. Guess I'll spend the night over in that cabin," I answered, pointing toward the other structure.

The older man scowled.

"Someone else is staying over there," he said. "And they'll be back soon."

Then, with a beckoning motion to the younger hunter, the older man retreated into the cabin. When both hunters were inside, the door was shut and neither spoke to me again.

I felt that my sudden appearance was an unwelcome one. In any case, I certainly did not care to spend any more time than would be necessary for rest. Relying on a hunch that the other cabin really was vacant, I decided to check it out. It was empty, and apparently had been for months.

The next morning I woke to the sound of rushing water outside my window and was delighted to discover clear skies overhead. Through a large picture window I saw most of the mountains surrounding Karluk Lake nine miles away. Light clouds sailed south high above those peaks, a clear indication that a northwest wind prevailed.

A northwestern often is a "fair-weather" wind during the spring season, and I hoped it would last until I reached the P&T camp at the other end of the lake. A southern storm would create large waves and prevent me from wading past brush that extends out to the edge of the water. My load was heavy, and I hoped I would not be forced to carry it through the tangled alder and willow patches above the lake.

Remembering my "neighbors" next door, I peered out of another window to see if they were stirring. They were not outside, and no smoke came from their stovepipe. I assumed that they had already gone hunting.

The Alaska bush is full of all types of people. There are trappers, hunters, guides, taxidermists, poachers, homesteaders, squatters, hermits, miners, fishermen, and even fugitives from justice. Most residents are rather sociable, but some are not. Depending on the season, some suffer from cabin fever while others starve for companionship. Kodiak is rather representative of the rest of Alaska in all of these respects.

Shouldering my pack shortly after breakfast, I continued upstream along the river, amid eddies and scattered willows laced with young spring sprouts. Early spring — fresh air, new growth, and clear skies — is a precious time for the Kodiak wilderness traveler. The country bursts to life as teeming flocks of song birds and waterfowl arrive from the south. I watched several groups of mallards and teal swim ahead of me on the river, until they finally flew back downstream. I felt satisfied being alone again in the bush.

The trail along the river was excellent most of the way to Karluk Lake. Only occasionally did I abondon the river because of poor trail, or to shorten the distance around bends. Eagles were numerous along the river, and I saw at least three foxes before mid-afternoon — a "cross" and two reds. As warm as the days were becoming, I expected to see Browns moving into the flats to dig for edible roots. But, although I kept a keen eye open, I failed to see any bruins that day. The country seemed void of bears. Because I had seen one Brown on the portage, and the two hunters had seen "lots of bears" during their spring hunt, this absence of bears, and even bear sign, puzzled me. However, when I was within a few miles of Karluk Lake, I began to understand why there were so few of the beasts around. Almost everywhere I looked, on tundra trails and amid brush, human tracks were in evidence, as if I had missed a Kodiak cross-country parade.

Obviously, the tracks were those of more hunters who were staying in another Fish and Wildlife recreation cabin by the mouth of Karluk Lake. I knew there were several hunters because of the different tread on the soles of their hip boots, and because there were different brands of cigarette butts on the trails. Any clear-thinking Brown Bear would smugly avoid this territory; it literally looked like it had been trampled by a corps of rabbit hunters.

Inexperienced hunters often attempt to hunt Browns this way, but they seldom succeed. Most experienced Kodiak hunters employ the standard "spot and stalk" method of hunting. The only time they walk cross-country is when traveling between camp and some pre-determined observation point from which they "glass" for bear, or between that point and the bear once a decision is made to stalk it. Human scent can linger for days, or even weeks in dry weather, and many Kodiaks will spook if they smell human scent along a trail. So it is best to avoid leaving scent unless absolutely necessary.

The sun had set, and the colors on the skyline were almost gone when I rounded the last bend before reaching the lake. I had looked in vain all afternoon for hunters. Now I could see a faint glimmer of a gas lamp shining through a cabin window. As I neared, I observed an angler casting in the river for trout. He was totally oblivious to my presence until I surprised him with a greeting.

"Hello," I said in a somewhat subdued tone. "Catch any fish?"

The man appeared surprised, but nodded, and then pulled two large rainbows from the water near his feet. They were beauties.

"Where did you come from?" he asked politely.

As I introduced myself to the fisherman, another figure appeared at the cabin, and through the open door I could see a third man reading a book by lamp light. The hunters were servicemen stationed in Alaska. Although enjoying a hunt they would remember all their lives,

19

they had killed no bear and indicated that they had made the tracks out in the flats. They invited me to coffee; so while sharing information, I explained the "spot and stalk" method as I had learned it from P&T. After more than an hour of story-telling, I shouldered my pack and retreated to the nearby Fish and Game research cabin for the remainder of the evening. Hopefully, I would be at the P&T camp on Karluk's south end by the next evening.

CHAPTER II

I had just eaten breakfast when I heard the sound of a light aircraft approaching from out over the flats. The plane buzzed overhead, tipped its wings, then circled and landed on the lake. It was one of the island's several bush pilots, and he stepped out onto the bird's float after it was close to shore.

"Are you the fellows who called for a plane?" he asked the three hunters who had assembled on shore ahead of me.

Evidently someone had called for a flight and the directions became confused; or, perhaps this was the pilot's way of checking on the Karluk hunters' health without embarrassing them. None of the men acknowledged calling for a plane.

"I don't know about anyone else wanting a ride, but I'd like to go up the lake to the P & T camp if you're heading that way," I said. "How much will you charge me?"

"Twenty dollars. Where is your gear?"

Twenty dollars sounded like a bargain. I explained that I needed to bring my gear from the Fish and Game cabin.

"How long?" he asked.

"Fifteen minutes."

"Too long," he said.

"Ten minutes?"

"Go get it!"

Unbelievably, I completed three trips from the State cabin in less than ten minutes. My pack had been unloaded, so I toted gear in my arms. The pilot enjoyed a cup of coffee with the hunters, shared the latest news from town, and then we were off to the south end of Karluk Lake. I was a little disappointed that I would miss the walk, but Kodiak weather is unpredictable, and I didn't want to take a chance on missing Pinnell at his camp. I hoped to arrive at the P & T camp in time to enjoy some good bear hunting.

The Cessna 206 thundered across the water and lifted us aloft. Minutes later we were almost within sight of our destination. Ducks were swimming on the surface of the lake below us; I saw several groups flying across the lake near shore. The plane descended gently when we neared the lake's south end.

"I was in here last week," the pilot yelled above the engine's roar. "They've got one hunter."

Very little snow remained on nearby peaks, but most of the trees had not put on new leaves. This year was a far cry from the last spring I hunted as an assistant guide for P & T. More than 60 inches of snow covered most slopes that year, and four feet of ice were on the lake. In fact, a ski plane landed on frozen Olga Bay — covered with *saltwater* ice — as late as May 1.

The craft bounced slightly when it touched water, and the pilot set it in smoothly to end our flight. We taxied to shore near the P & T cabin. Bill Pinnell and his entire outfit were waiting. The guide recognized me when I stepped out on the float and began pulling up my hip-waders.

"Well," he exclaimed, "who have we here?"

"Just me," I replied.

We were still drifting in three feet of water, and a rope was thrown to the men on shore. Stepping off the float, I waded to shore.

"Hello, Bill," I said. "Still hunting bears, I see."

Pinnell nodded and looked grim.

"I guess you could say we're *chasing* bears this year! We're having an awfully hard hunt because of the weather. It is warmer than usual, and the bears are already rutting. Most of these spring bears are rubbed bad, and the ones that aren't won't stay still long enough because of the rut."

Browns are extremely active during the rut, or breeding season. Only a fortunate hunter can get close enough to shoot one. Even in a normal year, some bears will demonstrate this activity in the early spring when they begin travelling cross-country. They plow through deep snow like bulldozers and move over mountain after mountain. The trails they leave in the snow are visible for miles.

We watched the Cessna disappear behind mountains. Then Pinnell instructed his troupe to assist me with my gear. I was assigned to a top bunk over where the hunter slept. I felt relieved to be back in familiar territory and felt comfortable in the small frame cabin. Lunch was almost ready, and Pinnell offered me coffee when I sat at the table.

"Morris had hunters at the cannery this year," he began, "and they had a hard hunt, too. But his hunters are finished, and we still have one to go."

Pinnell's hunter, a retired businessman from the west coast, had spent most of his life dreaming about hunting the big bear. Pinnell introduced me to the man, then began telling the story of how I came to Alaska.

"He was from St. Louis, and he was going trapping alone out in the Kuskokwim!" Bill chuckled.

Although I graduated from high school in St. Louis, I also grew up in Texas and Oklahoma. Since grade school, I had always been an avid fur trapper. I trapped muskrat, mink, raccoon, fox, and even a beaver or two from nearby ponds, streams and meadows. As I grew up, my trapping aspirations kept pace, and by my junior year in high school, I was determined to trap in Alaska. I discussed these plans with a fur buyer in St. Louis, and he told me that if I tried to go trapping in Alaska on my own, I would be a stiff when they dug me out of the ice and snow the next spring.

This man had hunted with P & T and scored a nice bruin. He gave me a letterhead he'd received from the guides, and suggested that I write and see about working for them for awhile before going out alone. I did this. To my surprise, I soon got a telephone call from

Pinnell, who told me to hurry up to the Great Land. Although interested, I wasn't too impressed with Kodiak as trapping country. The interior of Alaska is reputed to be much colder than Kodiak Island, and every trapper knows that the finest furs usually come from the coldest territory. I later learned that even Kodiak Island can be an icebox in the winter.

When I got off the plane in Anchorage, I had about $700 in my pocket, camp gear, and enough steel traps to string across the state. A missionary bush pilot who lived in Palmer, Alaska, had already reluctantly agreed to fly me out into the Kuskokwim basin, and then to check on me periodically. Because Pinnell also maintained a residence in Palmer, the two began trying to change my mind. Pinnell introduced me to many of his friends, including the town banker and a local magistrate, urging everyone to talk me out of going into the Kuskokwim alone. I wouldn't budge; so Pinnell soon gave up and headed into the Brooks Range to guide sheep hunters. I remained in Palmer and continued getting ready to move out into the bush.

Looking back, I really did a remarkable job outfitting my expedition. However, that dream was not to be. Just before casting off, I became badly ill with flu and strep-throat and did not recover for weeks. By that time, I wisely determined that there wasn't enough time to build a suitable cabin before winter would set in. So I sent P & T a note and asked if I could still have the job on Kodiak.

When Pinnell finished telling his version of how I wound up in Alaska, he turned to a more serious note.

"Looks like the wind is going to stay in the southeast this afternoon," he told his assistant guide. "Maybe you can take the hunter up Cascade Creek to the top of the pass and see if any bears are in the ravines there."

After lunch, we sat outside the cabin scanning distant slopes while Pinnell continued deliberating about a plan of action. When the old guide was sure that the wind would remain favorable, he gave his blessings to the assistant and watched the group depart. The hunter nonchalantly laid his rifle over one shoulder and walked into the brush between the assistant and packer.

"I don't know when I've met a better man to have in camp," Pinnell declared. "Some of those who *call* themselves hunters would be threatening to sue me over a poor hunt like this one. *Some* of those guys would be begging me to use an airplane to get them a bear. But this man seemingly enjoys just being out here. This is about the worst year I've ever seen, and if I live over it, I'll live to be an old, old man!''

Pinnell was anxious to see his hunter connect with a Brown, and the guide was doing every legal thing within his power to see that he did. Pinnell was familiar with hard hunts and was bravely facing facts.

"You can't afford to give up the hunt!'' he concluded.

I watched Pinnell react to the adverse conditions and listened to him bitterly protest the situation. Yet, this guide had faced disaster before, and he was not even wistfully considering the use of those airplane tactics employed by some poachers and unscrupulous guides.

I knew that Pinnell's partner, Morris Talifson, had reacted similarly on numerous occasions. In fact, Talifson once faced disaster during the most prestigious hunt of the entire P & T career without bartering fair chase for success. That 1967 hunt was with Prince Abdorezzi Pahlavi, brother to the late Shah of Iran.

In the spring of 1967, P & T stood at the height of their careers, their record book fame having literally spread world-wide as sportsmen from all parts of the globe came to hunt the magnificent Kodiak Brown Bear with equally outstanding guides. It was only natural that Prince Abdorezzi Pahlavi would choose the two to guide him to a pair of special-permit browns for his wildlife museum in Iran. After the two guides decided that Talifson would lead the foray, Talifson brooded for weeks over the question of where would be the best place to hunt. Talifson's Konaig packer still recalls those last days before the royal client arrived.

"Talifson, he sat around house long time deciding best place to take Prince,'' the Native said. "He wouldn't talk — just sat by stove smoking his pipe, looking out window — maybe week before hunt. Then one day, he said, 'We'll go to Fraser Lake, because that's where the big bear is.' ''

In this case, Talifson probably was demonstrating his uncanny ability to place mind over matter in a staunch, undying will to find a big bear for his client. This Kodiak bear guide, who at times seemingly thinks like a Brown Bear, perhaps has become the greatest Brown Bear hunter alive, and stands among the top of his prede-

25

cessors of long ago — those who've gone on to hunt in "The Great Beyond." But despite Talifson's deep deliberations and careful planning, events that would test his mettle soon developed.

The royal party went to Fraser in a ski plane that had landed on Akalura Lake near the Olga Bay camp. The big lake still was frozen, but covered with slush. For almost a week, the party did nothing but glass. Talifson spotted several nice trophies, but nothing in the 10-foot class. Although most of the snow was gone from lower slopes, and the rut was beginning to stir the hearts of many bears, for some reason the really big ones stayed back and refused to show. Before Fraser's ice became too rotten to walk on, the guide and his hunters worked from one end of the lake to the other, glassing canyons on both sides, from the middle of the ice. From 6 a.m. to 7 p.m., the men worked in ever-lengthening spring sunlight. With the start of a new week, Talifson began taking his client deeper into the heads of canyons, searching out every nook and cranny where a big bear might be lying.

Talifson recalls those days afield when he guided Prince Abdorezzi: "The prince was confident, and a good man to guide. He had hunted all over the world and understood what went into a successful hunt. Outside of the uncontrolled weather, my only concern was with his two photographers. They were good photographers, but every time we crossed a creek, or did something else that they wanted a picture of, we had to stop and let them get their cameras set up. It took forever to get anywhere, because of all the photography."

Even today, however, Talifson acknowledges the beautiful, professional accomplishments of the photographers on that hunt.

Talifson worked his hunters hard. More than one of his assistant guides has remarked about the man's ability to "walk a person into the ground." In the bush, a man must depend upon his feet for much transportation, and soon learns to walk fast. Such was the case with Talifson. Because the success of many hunts depended on his determination to round a mountain, or reach a point in time to cut off a bear's escape, the guide developed an extremely fast gait. Some have said that it takes "two good men," as it were, to keep up with him.

After 20 years to meditate on his own record book hunt with Talifson, William Hollinger, who took Brown Bear #114, made this statement: "It was Talifson's *will to win* that made him a great Brown

26

Bear guide. When all others would have given up on the trail, *he* kept them going, persistently pursuing their ultimate goal, the king-size Kodiak bear.''

As Talifson, the Prince and others made their way around Fraser country, looking, watching and waiting for an exceptional bruin to show itself, no one suggested that they bag less than the best trophy. The men worked through their second week, and, although two huge bruins were seen going over ridges into Red Lake country, neither was within range. So the hunters continued searching. When their second week ended, the big tickets still had not been filled. Talifson began a third week of hunting.

"We saw lots of bears," he explains. "Trouble was, there were none I wanted the Prince to shoot. One day I saw four nine-footers, but I knew it might only take one more day to see two tens. So we kept looking."

Finally, the party was down to the wire. The Prince could afford to hunt for months, but business demanded that he leave. May 15 had to be the last day. Talifson and the hunters glassed from a mountainside to the north of Midway Creek all morning. They'd just finished their lunch a little past noon, and the feeling prevailed that perhaps the Prince's business on the home front would cost him a successful hunt. But still the men hunted, never losing sight of the fact that a big Brown Bear usually is where you find it, and can appear at any moment.

While guiding the Prince, Talifson remembered those two ten-foot bruins taken by two of his earliest hunters — two bears that fell side by side — on the last day of a hunt. He remembered another record book hunt when two trophies were bagged in a single afternoon, after days of fruitless effort. He also remembered scores of other fine trophies — many of them ten, and even eleven-footers — that were taken on the last day of hunts after everyone but the guide had lost all hope. But Talifson never lost hope.

By now, the Prince was regretful that this was to be his last day in Brown Bear country. But he displayed calm determination to put full confidence in his guide, right up to the end, and to accept the outcome regardless of what it might be.

This seemingly fruitless hunt was Talifson's finest hour. No airplanes were used — not even to scout the territory for suitable trophies. No walkie-talkies were in his possession. The guide did not resort to any of the scandalous methods employed by some outfitters. Yet, there he sat on the mountainside with the most prestigious client of his entire career, looking total defeat straight in the eyes. However, not once was he tempted to trade fair chase for a "successful" hunt. Talifson simply was being himself, a guide's guide.

Then, Talifson's impelling will to win paid off. Suddenly, there on the south slope, just a little above the upper portion of Midway Creek, stood one of the biggest and best furred ten-foot brownies that the old guide had seen in a long, long time.

"There's a bear!" he cried, almost too loudly, but with the tearful emotion of an old prospector who'd just found the Mother Lode.

Seeing that spring beauty understandably excited Talifson and his royal client. There could be no doubt about the legality of such a huge bruin. Talifson customarily observes an animal several minutes before beginning any line of action, and this procedure removes much doubt about the bear's direction of travel. But the Prince waited three weeks without complaining, and finally the bear was there. Talifson knew the wind was favorable, and seeing little chance of the animal escaping from that box canyon without being seen, decided to begin the stalk.

"However," Talifson recalls today, "we were halfway down the mountainside when we passed a big clump of brush, and an eight-footer ran out of the alders up ahead — coming our way."

This second bear was completely unexpected and added a whole new dimension to the situation. When the Prince saw the animal, he raised his arm and waved at it as if to say, "Go back!"

"The bear stopped," Talifson remembers, "and looked at us, then continued our way. The Prince waved again, more forcefully. This time the bear stood up on its hind legs and stared at us, then slowly lowered itself and kept coming straight for us.

"I told him, 'It won't do any good to wave at it; the bear's going to keep coming. You may as well go ahead and shoot it.'

"Well, he didn't want to shoot the eight-footer, and it kept coming. By now, the bear was beginning to get close.

"'You better shoot it,' I urged, but the Prince didn't want to, and kept waving. The darned bear was getting right on us, and finally I heard it pop its jaws!

28

"'Shoot the bear!' I exclaimed. 'If you don't take it, it might take you!'

"So finally the Prince shot once, and the bear ran down into a gully and didn't come out.

"'Where did it go?' I asked.

"'It's dead,' the Prince calmly declared. 'Now we've lost the big bear.'

"'Don't worry about it,' I told him. 'We'll go on down there anyway, and he'll be there.'

"We were in a box canyon, and I knew the big bear probably would choose an escape route through the brush if it could," Talifson recalls. "So after checking the smaller bear, which was indeed very dead, I took the Prince down to where I thought I could set him up for the big one.

"'Now watch that little opening,' I told him, 'and the bear will pass right through it.'

"When the bear did walk through the opening, that was that, and both tags were filled. The Prince was an incredibly accurate shot. His first shot hit the bear in the shoulder and knocked it off its feet. The second shot killed it. The old boar squared ten feet, six inches, and placed very high in the Boone and Crockett record book."

As of this writing, more than fifteen years have passed since Talifson guided the Prince on that epic hunt; the great bear has been duly recorded and its proud owner rightfully lauded for his success in the field. But the experience symbolizes sportsmanship at its highest. Whenever I go afield in P & T territory, I am reminded of the story as it was told to me by Morris Talifson. Even as I sat in Bill Pinnell's camp at Karluk Lake, I contemplated its message, and concluded that in a poor season like the present one, true hunters can have success in the field.

The hunters were late returning that evening. I pitched in and helped the other packer in camp prepare supper for the hungry men before they returned. We all waited to learn whether the hunter had scored. Upon their return, however, we learned that they had endured near-blizzard conditions soon after reaching the top of the high-altitude pass. While we saw a slight drizzle rain at our low level during part of the afternoon, the sportsmen were engulfed in a cloud of snow on the pass. Despite this, all of the men were exuberant. They had

29

enjoyed watching two otters carrying on with antics for almost an hour.

"I had no idea that otters were so graceful!" the hunter declared.

I listened to the men recount their experience, and heard the master guide tell his own stories — to the accompaniment of sizzling embers in a Yukon stove. Inwardly, I concluded that regardless of its ultimate outcome, this hunt already was a success.

The camp was humming when I arose the next morning. Bill's assistant guide already had a fire going in the stove, and the smell of coffee and bacon permeated the room. The men didn't waste time getting started that day, because the weather was excellent, and the client's hunt would last only two more days. However, the man didn't score a Brown that day, and he finally faced the last day of his hunt. But, when the crew returned that evening, he still had downed no bear.

"Well," the hunter announced in a quiet tone when he returned from his last day afield, "we almost got a bear today. But while we were making our stalk, and couldn't see the bear's exact location, it moved downwind of us and caught our scent. We just caught a glimpse of its hind end disappearing through brush."

We were standing by the lake shore waiting for a chartered plane to land and carry the crew back to Olga Bay, when I heard the guide express his regret that the hunter had not scored. After we were back at the cannery and the hunter had left for town, Bill's admiration for the sportsman was fully expressed.

"That was one of the hardest hunts I believe I've ever seen," he said. "But the hunter's hunt was a success, because he enjoyed just being out there with the bears. In that respect, I can't say that the results were too bad."

CHAPTER III

The Olga Bay crew was elated by the success of their other clients. Two of Talifson's hunters bagged bruins that would qualify for listing in *Records of North American Big Game*, published by the Boone and Crockett Club. Several others scored well with smaller, but respectable, trophies. While Talifson supervised the assistant guides and packers who were busy fleshing hides and cleaning skulls, Pinnell sorted through piles of unopened letters from sportsmen seeking information about the next year's hunts.

"I make my living by answering letters from hunters," Pinnell said.

There is no way to estimate the exact number of letters that P & T have answered since they began guiding in 1949. They certainly must number in the tens of thousands. However, while their total mailings may be beyond estimate, the number of sportsmen they've guided, and the number of Kodiaks actually taken, are not. All told, P & T have guided over 1,000 sportsmen since they began. Some of their clients were fishermen and Arctic sheep hunters. But between the two guides, they probably have accounted for between 700 and 800 Kodiaks, an astounding number. Since the guides hunted together during some seasons, each can fairly estimate to have personally been on over 500 Kodiak bear hunts.

While a few other guides claim "*bear*-kill" records approaching that of P & T, without any exception known to this writer, those guides all operate in Black Bear territory where each hunter is allowed to take two or three blackies every year. Kodiak hunters are allowed to take only one Brown Bear every four regulatory years. So when a guide claims to have been in on a large number of "*bear*-kills," two-thirds of his record may consist of Black Bears. There are no Black Bears on Kodiak, and the number taken by P & T sheep hunters in the high Arctic probably can be counted on the fingers of two hands.

Even more astonishing than the total number of Brown Bears taken by P & T hunters, is the number of those taken which were large enough to be listed in the Boone and Crockett record book.

"We'd never even heard of the Boone and Crockett Club record book when we started guiding," Pinnell explains. "So we simply cut off the bears' heads and left them in the field to rot. Then Jonas Brothers of Seattle, now known as Klineberger Brothers, told us to start bringing in the skulls, because we were leaving a lot of big skulls out in the field that would make the book. Since then, our clients have accounted for one-third of all Kodiak Brown Bears listed in the record book."

The P & T record is simply astounding. As far as this writer has been able to determine, no other guides in Alaska's history have ever guided more Brown Bear hunters, or legally accounted for more Brown Bears, than these two. None has ever matched the P & T record book success, and probably none ever will. The Pinnell and Talifson record is a legacy for sport hunters that probably will stand for all time.

P & T haven't always been so successful, however.

"I grew up poor," Pinnell explains. "My dad was reliant and hard working but ran a truck farm near Sedalia, Missouri, and worked in the coal mines during the winter. I never went to school. I went to work in the coal fields when I was seven."

The bitterness of hard times — *real* hard times — gave Pinnell an extremely hard drive and pushed him forward. Morris Talifson also had a restricted background and was born on a homestead outside Bynum, Montana. His formal education was limited to the eighth grade, but no one who knows Morris can deny his marked intelligence.

"When I was nine," the master hunter reminisces, "my father lost the homestead in a drought. For more than two months our family of 10 kids lived almost entirely on rabbits, ducks and sharp-tailed grouse that I bagged."

Young Talifson already was becoming prepared for Kodiak at the

The author focuses his camera while resting along the Karluk River.

The author was charged twenty dollars for a lift to Pinnell's camp on Karluk Lake.

"Seeing bears and getting up on them are two different things," says Pinnell.

Hard hunting, but definitely "fair chase."

The author glasses for bears at Karluk Lake.

The world's biggest bear trail—four feet deep in places.

Some bear has been digging roots around here!

Beaver dam in the Ayakulik Flats.

The Ayakulik Flats.

The Ayakulik Flats are not hospitable in warm weather. If not eaten by mosquitoes, one can be swallowed by sink holes.

This old miner's cabin on Kodiak's south end is "hanging on for dear life."

A friendly Kodiak Red Fox.

The author, at age 18, takes a rest while packing his first ten-foot bear hide.

Inside the Silver Salmon cabin: the author's coffee-can stash of food was still there.

This ten-foot boar tipped the scales at nearly 1500 pounds. Any hunter who bags such a beast can expect to be excited. Photo courtesy of P & T collection.

Memorable moments: etched in time, but not lost to the past. Photo courtesy of P & T collection.

T.H. McGregor with prime Fall trophy. Although this hide measured only nine feet, the bear's skull was listed as number seven in the Boone and Crockett Club record book. The light-colored areas on the bear's flanks are not rubs, but are areas of thin fur in the animals "arm-pits". Photo courtesy of P & T collection.

P & T hunters with two ten-footers taken on the same hunt. Photo courtesy of P & T collection.

This Brown Bear placed very high in the Boone and Crockett Club record book. Note the left side of bear's neck, where it has small rub. Photo courtesy of P & T collection.

Years ago, P & T crews spent days packing gear into Fraser Lake each spring. Photo courtesy of P & T collection.

This P & T hunter took a fine reindeer while guided by Morris Talifson's nephew, Larry Talifson. Photo courtesy of P & T collection.

Morris Talifson with a <u>very</u> old bear taken by one of his hunters. Photo courtesy of P & T collection.

Oregon hunter with eight-foot six-inch trophy taken on his second hunt. The beautifully-furred November trophy was taken north of Olga Bay.

"Slamming Sammy" Snead, right, and his son Jack, left, with Jack's nine-foot Kodiak. This prime trophy was taken on a November hunt.

Bill Pinnell and Morris Talifson pose with a big boar. Photo courtesy of P & T

age of nine!

In 1923, after a two-year stint with Swift & Company, 25-year-old Pinnell and Bob Slowe began raising foxes and skunks in the rugged foothills of Missouri's Ozark Mountains. After two successful seasons there, the two fur farmers decided Montana climate was much better for raising fur. So they relocated in Montana on 13 acres they rented from a dairy farm near Choteau.

"Our new farm just blossomed," says Bill, "and we opened two raw fur offices to boot. I began going into the sticks to buy fur, and that's when I met Morris."

Pinnell offered the 16-year-old trapper a job feeding stock on his fur farm, and Morris accepted. When, in 1927, Bob Slowe decided to quit fur farming, Morris and Bill bought Bob's share in the business. The two have been partners ever since.

"Morris and I succeeded as fur farmers two more years," Bill continues. "And in 1929 we had a net worth of $30,000, a lot of money in those days. When the depression started that year, we didn't even know the meaning of the word 'depression.' I was buying sheep and cattle hides that year. Prices were falling as the economy went bad. I could buy all of those skins I wanted for just 25 cents apiece, and that's what I did — expecting a big profit. But when I sent several truckloads of my 25-cent skins to market, the hides didn't even pay their own freight. I had lost both of our shirts in one swoop! By 1930 we were worth only $15,000, and at the end of 1931 we were broke. Morris and I had $200 and a 1928 Chevy. We bought two gold pans and two shovels, and headed for the West Coast. I told Morris, 'If worse comes to worse and we have to stand in a soup line, nobody will know us.' We were broke but couldn't give up."

The Great Depression began six long years of drifting around the Northwest for Pinnell and Talifson. They tried regaining their lost status, but simply fumbled for things to do.

"We mined and picked hops and fruit in season," Talifson recalls. "We even tried to be woodcutters one year, but that didn't work out because Bill accidently broke our only saw and we were busted again!"

Pinnell and Talifson heard about gold mining near Roseburg, Oregon, and spent most of their lean years there, mining gold on the banks of "Cow Creek." P & T concede that it was at Cow Creek that they became the men they are today, enduring hardships and working hard with little promise of return. Bill Pinnell remembers that Cow Creek also was where he first began hunting as a form of livelihood, feeding Morris and himself, as well as most of the other unfortunates they met.

"Those poor old souls got $1.50 a week welfare," he explains, "and that little bit went just about as far as it could go. But still they had no meat. Somebody came along and put up signs across the river that said 'No Hunting, No Hunting, No Hunting.' But that was the best deer hunting I ever had!"

Bill waited until dark to return from these hunts, and usually a crowd of hungry miners were gathered at P & T's tent, standing in line, waiting for the future bear guide to divide his kill.

"We saw bread selling for four cents a loaf, but couldn't buy because we didn't have four cents!" Pinnell declares today. "The soles of our shoes were worn through and padded with cardboard, but that was mighty good walking in those days, I must say!"

P & T returned to Montana for a brief visit in 1938, and an old friend told them of reading about a place he called "Kodiak." Hearing the man's story got Bill to thinking, and soon the two were headed north for Alaska!

"We knew Charlie Buroaker had gone to Alaska two years before, and had made $500 in one winter mining gold on the south end of Kodiak," Bill reminisces. "We figured we'd do better than that in the summer."

So it was six years of hard times and the centuries-old lure of gold that caused P & T to head north. On July 5, 1938, Pinnell and Talifson landed at Seward, Alaska, having paid $41 steerage. After securing temporary employment on a freighter, the pair worked their way to Kodiak, and soon hitched a ride around the island on a mail boat.

"Boats were the only form of transportation here in the old days," Pinnell remembers. "And when we landed, we didn't know a soul."

During the last week of July, P & T set foot on the head of Olga Bay, on what has to be one of the most desolate, wind-blown pieces of real estate in Alaska. Flat and boggy, with no windbreaks, this arctic taiga receives the brunt of howling North Pacific storms year-round. For three years the men lived in a "barabara"-type shack at the mouth of Red River, eking out a living from gold-bearing black sand.

"Then one day," says Bill, "a friend dropped by and told us about a job he thought we should have. We were helping U.S. Fish & Wildlife at their Ayakulik River weir by that time, but this man felt we should be watchmen for the Alaska Packers' Association cannery in Olga Bay.

"'Why I don't know how to get that job,' I told him.

"'Well, if you want the job, I can get it for you,' he said.

"Several days later, the man sent word that said, 'Come on over, the job is yours.'"

Pinnell and Talifson finally had found their rainbow, and though they didn't realize it at the time, they were set for life. During World War II, both served as coast watchers, weir attendants, and enforcement officers for U.S. Fish & Wildlife; but after the war ended they were able to use this cannery arrangement to their advantage as guides.

"We had buildings for our hunters' quarters, office, cookhouse, bunkhouse, hidehouse and storage," Pinnell explains. "In the summer we have running water. And we have electric lights, too. We couldn't have asked for a better set-up."

There were several guides on Kodiak when P & T took their first hunters in the spring of 1949. And there still was plenty of open territory for newcomers. However, there was not so much open land that P & T could escape strong opposition from rivals. Fish & Wildlife agents in Kodiak, for whom the two had worked as weir attendants, originally encouraged Pinnell and Talifson to become guides, and simply issued them full guides' licenses the first year.

"But," says Bill, "another guide heard about the action and understandably took offense. He contested it and got us knocked back to assistant status. Then he showed up at the cannery and offered us jobs as assistant guides."

"'Well,' I said, 'I want to think about it.'

"'Well,' he said, 'Don't think too long, because I've got someone else in mind.'

"His offer sounded good," says Bill more than 30 years later. "But Roy Lindsley, the U.S. Fish & Wildlife agent who took the world's record bear, came along and I told him about the offer.

"'There's a sticker in it somewhere,' I said, 'and I can't see it.'

"'I can show you where the sticker is!' he said.

"'Where?'

"'He would have given each of you a hunter apiece. And he would have written straight to Juneau saying, 'I gave them two hunters;

51

they're not guides and never will be guides,' and your geese would have been cooked!'

"Now that guide was no dummy," says Bill. "He was thinking and planning ahead. Well, we didn't take his hunters that fall."

Pinnell and Talifson hired another guide to be offically in charge of their new operation until the two were able to obtain full guides' licenses. From that time forward no one could stop them from hunting on "their" end of Kodiak Island. P & T were triumphant. Their "inexorable will to win" finally had won. And the two were prepared to begin their careers as Kodiak Brown Bear guides.

"But," says Pinnell, "since we started guiding, we've learned that the business isn't always glamorous; guiding usually is a lot of hard work. For instance, the letters I type to hunters. Well, there's no end to the number of letters from people who want to hunt the big bear. Fortunately, we're limited in the number of bears we can take, so that limits the number of hunters, too."

Over the years, P & T have guided just about every sort of hunter a guide can imagine, ranging from royalty to auto mechanics, and from ministers to Chicago gangsters and a few others of questionable character.

"I once guided a cattle rancher who cancelled his check after leaving Olga Bay with a beautiful ten-foot bear hide," Pinnell remembers.

Although angered, Bill has only mildly considered using the same method of operation to even the score.

"I've often thought," he explains, "that it would be fun to go down there and buy one of his registered bulls — and then to cancel the check after we get the bull all the way up here in Alaska!

"Oh, we've seen them all. I've even had hunters with table manners so bad that not even a packer could tolerate them. Like the hunter who sent his piece of steak back to the kitchen for more cooking before reaching across the table and taking mine for himself — right off my plate — just as I was about to cut my first bite!"

As unsavory as a few hunters may hāve been, perhaps none has left the two guides with such utter frustration as did a father and son team that arrived one October. Although both got bears in only two days, the length of their visit was still *too* long.

"The first day we hunted," Pinnell recalls, "they woke me up at three a.m. I thought somebody was sick. But it turned out that the son, in his late twenties, wanted to show me his targets! He'd sighted in his rifle before they came up to Alaska, so he brought out his targets and laid them on the kitchen table, one by one. I stood there in my long-handle underwear — trying not to act out of the ordinary.

"'This one was shot at prone,' he said pointing at a target, 'and this one was shot kneeling, and this one was shot from a rest....'"

Pinnell was rightfully disturbed by the pair already this first morning, but the guide contained his indignation.

When Talifson arrived at five, he informed the men they'd be going to Akalura, and maybe the south end of Red Lake as soon as the sun came up.

"But," adds Talifson, "we took the father up towards the lake, and he couldn't make it walking so we took him in the boat down to Little Dog Salmon and he got a bear there. It was a 7½-footer."

"Then the next day," continues Pinnell, "they came over and woke me up again at three a.m. to ask for coffee! Well cripes! That time I told them I was used to sleeping in until an hour before sun-up. I went ahead and made them coffee, but after that I locked the front door at night. The old man would come over for coffee, at 3 a.m., and stand outside the door pacing back and forth until he gave up."

Talifson took the son to Red Lake the second day, and there connected with a beautiful 10-foot bruin.

"We were glassing at the south end of Red Lake," says Talifson, "and along about 3 o'clock in the afternoon, I spotted a big bear coming down off the hill on the east side. It was a heck of a big bear, and it lay down on an open knob just above the brush."

Talifson, hunter, and assistant guide started for the bruin. They walked around the gravel lake shore until several hundred yards directly below the animal, then cut up the hill. Talifson wanted to get level with or slightly above the beast before moving any closer. The men worked their way up through scattered alders and high grass, climbing slowly and glassing the animal often, lest they make some mistake that would alert the creature to their presence.

Just halfway up, Talifson saw the bear get up from the knoll and head downhill toward the lake.

The guide stopped, looked at the bear moving down the mountain, then turned to his assistant and said, "Go ahead and take the hunter on over. You can travel faster, and if the bear doesn't stop when it gets to the bottom, maybe you can catch it before it moves on."

"But," remembers Talifson, "they got over above the bear and it was still feeding down along the lake shore, so I caught up with them and we went on down."

The animal was slightly more than 100 yards from the hunters. There was a small strip of brush, and the bear was feeding behind that, next to the beach. Talifson told the hunter to shoot.

"The first shot, I think the son missed the bear; the second shot, he got it," says Talifson. "It was a big 10-footer."

So Talifson began skinning the animal, and had his assistant go to the lake's south end and get the boat that the outfit kept there. Then the hunter started poking around the bruin looking for bullet holes. He found the hole from his second shot.

"'Wonder where the other hole is?' he asked me," says Talifson.

"'I don't think there is another hole,' I said. 'Your first shot missed.'

"'Well, there ought to be another hole.'

"The hunter looked and looked for that other hole, but there wasn't one.

"'You missed it,' I said.

"No, he was sure he hit the bear both times. We skinned the animal, and turned the carcass completely over. There was only one hole in it. So then he began claiming he'd hit the bear in the same spot both times.

"'You missed it!'

"'No, I couldn't have!'

"Well, he wouldn't be convinced that he hadn't hit the bear both times. So I just dropped it. Several weeks later he sent me a letter. He and his father had flown to Seattle and driven the rest of the way home. The son said they were driving through Utah, and he saw a mountain that looked just like the one where we'd gotten his bear. He climbed up on that mountain, and there was a rock about the same distance as he'd been from the bear, and he shot at the rock. He said he 'couldn't possibly have missed the bear, because he hit the rock both times.' He had screwball ideas like that!"

Talifson finished skinning the hunter's bear, the assistant returned with their boat, and the party returned to Olga Bay. The father and son stayed around the cannery several days more. They fished for Dollies in the lagoon and relaxed while P & T took care of their trophies. Talifson observed the men as they drifted about the buildings snapping pictures of this, that, and another peculiarity, and though the real headaches they'd cause the outfit hadn't yet begun, he began to get some insight into the son.

"They were out fishing in the lagoon one day," Talifson says, "and it began sprinkling a little bit. So the father went into the hunter's quarters and brought out raincoats, telling his 28- or 29-year-old son, 'Here, sonny; don't forget to put on your raincoat!' just like he was talking to a three-year-old kid! Maybe he just needed to get away from Daddy."

Finally the day came when the hunters boarded a Kodiak Airways Widgeon for their return flight to town. They'd had photos taken of them with their hides, and requested the hides be shipped to their taxidermist when cured. The skulls were boiled clean and shipped directly to their homes several days later.

"But, several weeks later," says the guide, "the son wrote and said he hadn't received his skull. Bill wrote the man and told him the head had been mailed. Well, he looked around, and what had happened was that his mother-in-law had gotten ahold of it, stuck the skull away in a closet, and hadn't told him about it.

"Well, then the son wrote and claimed it wasn't his head. He had taken a picture of it with all the flesh still on — before it was boiled — and when it was boiled clean, the skull didn't look the same. He claimed his photo showed one tooth missing. So I wrote to him and explained that some of the teeth had been covered with dark deposits of tartar and other stuff, and that the boiling had left them all clean. I explained to the hunter that it *was* his skull.

"Not long after that I started getting all sorts of letters from people the son was writing to. He wrote several of the other hunters who were here at the same time and accused them of stealing his skull. He wrote to the taxidermist and asked him if he had it. He was causing a lot of static. Then I got another letter from him, and he accused me of lying. He said I'd sent his skull to the wrong people and he was going to write back to the taxidermist and all the rest of our hunters until he found out which one had it.

"Well, our livelihood depends on satisfied clients, and this man was causing our other hunters a lot of grief. They were all upset over the things he was accusing them of. So I wrote back to the man and told him to '*cut that out!*' I explained to him again that it was his skull, and told him what the difference was, and for him not to be upsetting all the other people by writing them nasty letters.

"Then the son wrote me another nasty letter, accusing me of lying to him, and said he was going to go tell some 'captain' what I had said. He swore up and down that he hadn't received his skull and one of those other people had it and wouldn't admit it.

"Things seemed to die down after that. My assistant saw the man in Anchorage several years later, and he still swore that it wasn't his skull. I don't think we've ever had any other hunters quite like those two."

Although P & T certainly have experienced a few frustrating situations down through the years that were caused by "kooky" hunters, the two have enjoyed far more hunter experiences that were — frankly — quite humorous.

"We had one old fellow who was a doctor from back east," Pinnell chuckles, "and this old guy called the hunter's quarters his 'office'! He always felt fine when the weather was too rough for hunting. But as sure as the sun shone, he'd have some ache or pain that kept him from hunting.

"The night 'Doc' arrived in camp, Morris and I told him we wanted to take him to Bare Lake the next day. But the next morning, Doc came into the house moaning and groaning. I asked him, 'What's the matter, Doc?'

"'Oh,' he said, 'I've got the darnedest toothache I've ever had!'

"'Well, don't you have anything for it?'

"'No,' he said, 'I didn't bring any pain killer and I think I ought to stay around here today.'

"I said, 'Well, whatever you think Doc.'

"The weather was *beautiful* that day. But during the night, a big storm blew up, and the next day was terrible for hunting. It was just too rough. Doc came prancing into the house that morning.

"'If it were a nice day,' he said, 'we could sure go hunting today! My toothache is a lot better.'

"'Well,' I said, 'it doesn't look like it's going to be any good today.'

"So Doc sat around the house all day visiting with us. We had a good time talking about medicine and just about everything you can think of. But we were hoping to get Doc out into the field the next day.

"Well, the next day was better for hunting. So when Doc didn't show up for breakfast, we sent the packer after him. A little while later, Doc came in. He looked terrible!

"'What's the matter, Doc?' I asked.

"'Oh,' he said, 'I've got the worst case of piles I've ever seen.'

"'Well, don't you have anything for it?'

"'No, I don't — this is a bad case — I think I'll stay in camp today.'

"I thought Doc was having bad luck, but the next day he came in again — moaning and groaning.

"I said, 'What's the matter, Doc?'

"He said, 'My back was hurt in an accident some time back, and I've got a disc that's acting up.'

"Well, then I started to wonder. I didn't know if he had a back ache or not! We sat around the house that day, and the next day his back still hurt him so we stayed in camp again. That night I told him, 'Doc, you need to get out and do some hunting before your hunt runs out.

"Well, Doc didn't say much, and the next day started out with terrible weather. Ol' Doc came into the house bright and early, just singing and dancing!

"'My,' he said, 'If it were a good day today we could sure go hunting. I feel ever so fine!'

"Well, this time Doc was caught in his own trap, because I looked out the window and I saw a little patch of blue opening up in the clouds!

"I said, 'Doc, it's clearing off outside. Now you and Morris get yourselves in gear and go try to find a bear!

"He was dragging his heels, but finally we got him ready and he and Morris started up the trail toward Akalura. They hadn't gone far when I looked out the window again, and there was a bear coming around the mountainside right above camp. So I ran up the board walk after them.

"'Now Doc,' I said, 'this is your chance. Let's get you up there to that bear and see if you can get it.'

"As we were starting for the bear, I saw it lie down above our water tank, so we went down the beach before starting to climb up to it. We got Doc up on the hill, just about level with the bear. It was only about 100 yards away. Doc sat down. He had a 'unipod' he was carrying—he took that out and poked it into the ground, then laid his rifle across the top to take aim.

"'Shoot it!'

"'Where?'

"The bear was lying with its side to us. I said, 'Shoot it in the chest.'

"Well, Doc shot. The first time he shot the bear, he missed it. The second time he hit it in the same place. The bear was up by then, and Doc was injecting a third shell into his rifle.

"'You're gonna have to do better than that,' I said. 'The bear is going to get away.'

"Doc shot again, and this time the bear went down, hit. He continued firing and finally killed the bear.

"We walked over to the bear, which had gone down in a hole between two large grass tussocks; it didn't look very big the way it was lying.

"'Why that's nothing but a cub!' Doc exclaimed when he saw the bear. 'I won't have it!'

"'That's a bigger bear than you think, Doc,' I said.

"'Why, I've killed 26 bears, and that's nothing but a cub! I won't have it.'

"So I had Morris, and a helper who'd just come up the hill, skin out the bear. Then I said to Doc, 'Doc, while they're skinning, let's go down to the house and have a drink.'

"We went down to the house, and after a couple of hours Morris came in too. He went into the other room to turn on the radio. I went in there with him and asked how big the hide was.

"'It squared out nine and a half feet,' he said.

"So then I went back to Doc.

"'Let's go out and take a look at that bear,' I said. 'That's a bigger bear than you think.'

"So we went out to the hidehouse, and Morris had the skin lying near the others we'd taken that fall. Ol' Doc stood there a second, looking at his bear's hide, rubbed his chin, then ran around it several times.

"'Dog-gone it, Billy! You're right! I'll kick one of those other bears out! I'll have it! I'll have it!'

"Then, a little while later the refuge manager landed at the cannery to put seals on all the hides and skulls. Doc ran out there to show him his hide. Boy, was he proud!

"'I'll have it,' he said," says Pinnell with a chuckle, "'I'll have it.'"

CHAPTER IV*

As Pinnell settled down to his typewriter and began answering the latest batch of hunters' letters, I wandered out to the hidehouse where Talifson and the hired help were doing their own share of the work. I found the crew sitting on boxes in a big circle around a bear hide. The scene reminded me of numerous occasions when, as an assistant guide, I took part in caring for such skins. I also recalled how the job really starts in the field, just as soon as a big bear is killed.

When a Brown Bear is downed, it is rolled over onto its back — belly up — and the toil begins. An incision is made from the throat of the bruin, starting between the jaw sockets and running down the center of its chest, all the way to its tail end. Probably most guides extend this cut all the way to the bear's anus, and then on out to the tip of its tail. However, P & T make it their practice to end the belly cut about six to ten inches from the anus. On a really big bruin, say about a 10½-footer, the belly cut may be ended almost 12 inches from the anus. But as a rule it is never ended less than six inches from the anus even on a small bear. The reason for doing this will become apparent in a moment.

After the other guides have extended their belly cut out to the tip of the tail, they begin hind leg cuts at the anus, or base of the tail,

This chapter contains much technical, but necessary information on caring for hides.

59

and slice the hide along the back, or rear side of the bear's leg, all the way to the back of its heel. Then, they cut around the inside edge of the rear paw pad to the base of the bear's toe pads. Later, if the hide is made into a rug, the bottom edge of the rug will be contoured, so that its shape resembles the natural curves of the bear's hind legs.

P & T, on the other hand, end their belly cuts about six to ten inches up from the anus; then they make a cut straight out the *inside* of each hind leg, all the way to the edge of the heel, before cutting around the inside edge of the bear's rear paw pad to the base of the toe pads. Consequently, if the hide is made into a rug, the bottom edge of the rug will be straight across, giving the skin a "square" appearance. The hide also will be a little longer than it would have been if the leg cut had begun at the anus. This is because belly skin that would have been attached to the sides of the hide above each hind leg, is attached to the bottom of the skin instead. Although fewer guides skin bears this way, the practice is by no means uncommon. It has been in use ever since sport hunters began shooting the big Browns in Alaska, as is demonstrated by hunting books dating back to around the turn of the century. Any experienced taxidermist recognizes this method of skinning Brown Bears.

P & T ship their "square-skinned" hides to virtually all major taxidermy firms in the U.S. They usually recommend to the taxidermists that the tail be removed from where it is naturally attached (about six to ten inches from the bottom of the hide), and replaced on the bottom edge of the skin. When the anus hole is sewn closed, no one can tell that the tail has been moved. This writer, however, prefers to have the tail left in its natural position with the anus sewn closed beneath it.

After the belly and hind leg cuts have been completed, two more cuts are made. These are from the center of the bear's chest, between the front legs, down the inside of each front leg to the base of each front paw. Then the skin is slit around the inside edge of each front paw pad, to the base of the toe pads. *Notice*, that just as is done on the hind paw pads, this latter cut is around the *inside* of each front paw pad. This is *crucial* if the bear is to be mounted life-size, because stitches on the finished trophy will be less noticeable if they are on the inside edge of the paw pad.

The bottoms of the hind feet usually don't show even if mounted life-size. But, depending on the bear's pose, they might be visible. So the cuts are always made along the inside edge of the paw pads.

Because hunters frequently decide to have their trophies mounted life-size after they have already been skinned, P & T follow the prudent practice of leaving all paw pads attached to the hide along their outside edge. A cut is made across the bottom of each paw at the base of the toe pads — from the inside of the paw to the outside edge. Then the pad is simply laid back toward the outside edge of the paw as the bottom of each paw is skinned.

When all of the basic body cuts have been made, most of the remaining chore is a matter of peeling the hide back with the help of a sharp skinning knife — just like you'd peel a banana. If the hide must be packed a great distance, guides sometimes will "skin it close," so that most of the fat is left on the carcass. However, if the distance is not great, and especially if daylight is short, the hide shouldn't be skinned too closely, because it is too easy to "scour" it by cutting into the hair roots. Whenever a hide is "scoured," the fur in that spot will be lost in tanning. The fur will "slip" during tanning, causing bald spots wherever the skinner cut into the hair roots, just like it would if the hide were allowed to "taint."

The author received a letter from a bear hunter who complained that an assistant guide on the Alaska Peninsula ruined one side of his bear hide by skinning it too closely. The man saw what the assistant was doing and warned him, but the warning fell on deaf ears. Although the assistant apparently did not cut all the way through the hide, he skinned it so closely that massive areas of roots were cut, and consequently the trophy was seriously damaged.

As the skin is peeled back, it is dislocated from the bear's carcass in several spots. Each toe bone is dislocated at the joint between the foot pad and toe pad. The tail bone also must be chopped unless the tail is split and skinned on the spot. If the hide is "square-skinned" the carcass must be reamed around the intestine connected to the anus. This intestine is then chopped off a couple of inches inside the body cavity so that the anus hole will be as small as possible.

Finally, when the hide is severed from the feet and hind-end, it is drawn forward, over the bear's head; then, the neck is dislocated at a large joint just below the skull. Some guides will completely skin the head before severing it from the body. This is not wise if the bear is skinned late in the day with little light; because the eyes are so easily damaged when being skinned, they require special care. However, if the hide must be packed a great distance, and is a large one, weight can be distributed more evenly between two packs by separating the hide from the skull. A pack containing a single, good-sized skull, along with other gear, can weigh well over 50 pounds, so spreading the load often is necessary.

Another point to remember after the bear is skinned is that the skin should be cooled to remove body heat before it is rolled up for any length of time. This is because a bear's fur is very efficient insulation, and the temperature on the inside of the bundle will be very slow to change to match that on the outside. If the hide is full of body heat when it is rolled up, that warmth will be trapped on the inside of the bundle, and the skin may taint, causing hair slippage in the same manner as that caused by "scouring." Common sense is required in judging how long is long enough, but the hide should not feel warm. Usually, if only one experienced skinner is working the carcass, most of the hide will be cool before the job is finished.

If it is impossible to skin the bear on the same day it is shot, the bruin should be completely gutted. Then the chest cavity should be braced open with stout sticks, so that cool air can circulate inside the carcass. The bear should be rolled onto its chest, so its back side also will be exposed to cool air. *Do not* leave the bear on its back overnight, because heat will be trapped between the bear and the ground, and tainting may occur.

P & T probably have skinned more Brown Bears than any two men alive. But they've also become very efficient in caring for their hides after they're skinned. I watched the P & T crew, while they sat in a big circle around their hunter's trophy, "turning" its toes, eyes, ears, lips and nose. Their work was tedious, because each of these tender parts requires special care.

As indicated earlier, when a bear is skinned, each toe is severed at the joint between the toe and foot pad. When a skull is skinned, the eyes, ears and nose are skinned as close to the skull bone as possible in order to avoid damaging them. For the same reason, the lips are skinned close to where they join the gums on the inside of the bear's mouth.

Because these tender areas would not otherwise permit penetration of salt, the hide must be "turned" or "split," and then fleshed to remove the fat found there. The hide around each toe bone is also turned, almost out to the claw, and fleshed. Then, salt is worked in around each toe bone, under the skin. Likewise, the nose must be "turned" inside out, or skinned away from the gristle inside it, all the way out to the end, then fleshed and salted. The same procedure follows for the ears. The nose and ears should be left turned inside out and heavily salted for maximum penetration. P & T pour a large mound of salt over the entire head of each hide.

The eyes and lips of a bear hide are the most tedious portions to care for. These areas are lined with very tender skin. When the hide is laid flat — flesh side up — the tender skin that rolls over from the fur side in each of these areas, is the part that must be peeled back, or "split," so the area beneath it can be fleshed. A small, sharp blade is the only tool that will handle these delicate areas. Extreme care must be taken to avoid cutting holes in the lips or eyes. Excellent light and good vision are essential.

P & T usually care for these delicate areas while out in the hunting camps, during slack time. The remainder of each hide ordinarily is not fleshed in the field, because Talifson usually fleshes all hides over a beam at the cannery anyway. Consequently, the two guides usually wait until they return to the cannery to apply salt, too. The hides remain loosely rolled in a cool, dry place, until the time comes to fly them back to the cannery. Then, they usually are placed inside of large, heavy-duty canvas bags in order to keep grease, etc. from getting on everything else in the plane.

When I worked for P & T, if canvas bags were in short supply, the hides sometimes were flown back to the cannery inside of large plastic bags that were supplied by a major taxidermy firm. Hunters often use plastic bags for transporting hides longer distances, but several words of caution are in order at this point. First, always allow body heat to leave the hide before bundling. Second, never *seal* a hide inside a plastic bag unless the hide is to be frozen. Third, keep the plastic-bagged hide out of the sun's rays, because the sun will create a greenhouse effect inside the bag.

Personally, when forced to cover bear hides with plastic, I have always used sheet plastic, and have simply folded it loosely around the hide to keep the rest of my gear from getting greasy. Such a bundle, of course, is not airtight, because it is ventilated at all four corners. This, in my opinion, is just as safe an arrangement as any heavy-duty, tightly-woven canvas bag. In any event, always allow the hide to become as cool as possible, and put it in the shipping container only at the last minute before transporting it.

Some taxidermists claim that a bundled bear hide will "generate its own heat" inside the bundle, and that tainting will result. I have never engaged in any official scientific experiments to determine the validity of this claim. But I suspect that any hide that "generates its own heat" has not been properly cooled before being bundled. Anyone who has ever thawed a turkey for Thanksgiving knows that the center of the big bird is the last to thaw. Anyone who has ever frozen ice cubes knows that the center of the cube is the last to freeze. A cold object normally gets warm on its outside before warming up on the inside, and vice versa when cooling a warm object. Fur is an excellent insulator, and should retard warming of the center of a bundled bear hide. If a hide has been thoroughly chilled before being bundled fur side out, it's hard to see how the center of the hide can generate any heat before being thoroughly heated from without — and heated to the point that the growth of bacteria would create additional warmth. If any bundled hide will "generate its own heat," merely because of its great bulk, then it would be risky *ever* to "bundle" a hide that has not been thoroughly cured. In my opinion, if any tainting is to occur, it will take place in those areas nearest the outside of a bundled hide long before it happens at the core.

If bad weather prohibits flying the hide back to the cannery within a reasonable period of time, then P & T proceed to flesh it over their knees in camp. The hides simply are hung over the guides' knees while they slice away fat with sharp knives.

The dilemma of whether or not to actually flesh a hide in camp, as opposed to waiting until there is access to a fleshing beam, is a question frequently confronting guides and hunters. One must weigh all of the determining factors such as temperature and the lapse of time when making the decision. The general rule is that a hide should always be fleshed and salted *as soon as possible*. Unreasonable delay can result in a tainted hide. However, as long as the weather is cooperative, there is some leeway if immediate care is impossible. An experienced person can gauge the temperature, and by keeping a close eye on the hide, can properly determine how long it can reasonably wait for fleshing and salting.

Generally speaking, a bear hide will last without tainting for about as long as a piece of steak will last without tainting under the same conditions. If the hide begins tainting, the hunter should be able to recognize the symptoms and take immediate corrective actions. A tainted hide usually may take on a tainted odor, it may turn green, and its fat may become yellowish and appear sour. If kept dry, out of the sun, and in a cool environment no warmer that the low forties, an unfleshed and unsalted hide should remain in good shape for at least several days until proper care can be provided. However, P & T have kept unsalted hides in the field even longer without adverse effects when unable to care for them sooner.

"I had at least one hide," Talifson recalls, "that I kept out in the hunting camp without salting for a number of days when the weather wasn't too cold. I didn't feel very good about it; but, to my knowledge, the hide didn't spoil, and it came out okay. That was a situation that couldn't be helped under the circumstances."

Even if a hide is fleshed "over the knee" and salted out in the camps, Talifson fleshes it again over the fleshing beam at the cannery. This is because there is a thin layer of fat on a bear hide that is very difficult to remove with an ordinary knife; it is almost always left behind by even the best "knee-flesher." This layer of fat should be removed prior to salting if the hide is to cure properly. As far as this writer knows, P & T never have lost a hide due to tainting, probably because Talifson's methods of curing hides are so effective. In any event, one must be careful to prevent tainting, because the fur on a tainted hide will "slip," leaving bald spots on the fur side, the same way it would if the skin were "scoured" by a skinning or fleshing blade.

After Talifson's workers finished "turning" the delicate areas of the hide that was spread before them, Talifson directed them to drape it over his fleshing beam. Talifson's fleshing beam is approximately ten feet long and about ten inches in diameter. Several nails were used to tack the hide tightly to the beam. Talifson then took his 18-inch draw knife from the wall and began slicing fat away from the area of the skin that was over the beam. He worked with the grain of the hide, moving his draw knife from the head toward the tail.

When the area over the beam was clean of fat, the nails were removed, and the hide was shifted so that a new area could be fleshed. Talifson took great care to avoid fleshing the skin too closely; but he worked rapidly and with a deliberateness that should be practiced only by the most experienced flesher.

When the entire hide was fleshed clean of fat, it was taken to a vacant spot on the hidehouse floor where it was spread flat, fur side facing down. Talifson and the workers tacked it firmly to the floor, pulling the hide tight from all angles (but not stretching it). Then they buried the skin in more than an inch of salt. The average bear hide requires about a half pound of salt for each pound of hide if a thorough curing is desired.

The salt was carefully worked into the hide, and was packed into each toe, ear, the nose, and over the lips and eyes. When it was fully salted, the hide was measured. Then, a cardboard tag bearing its measurements and hunter's shipping instructions was tied to the skin.

Few hunters realize that successful Brown Bear hunts actually render two trophies. Second to the hide itself, a hunter also gets a skull. After Talifson and the crew finished caring for the hides, they descended upon the pile of bear skulls that had been waiting for them in another building. These were trimmed of meat and fur, and placed in five-gallon cans to boil in water and cleanser solution. About a pint of cleanser was added to each can. Because the cleanser had bleach in it, the solution cut grease and bleached the bone white at the same time.

Care must be taken not to boil skulls too long, because this loosens teeth and dissolves natural cement that bonds seams in skull bone. Talifson advises that skulls be boiled only long enough to cook and loosen the meat. Then, after the meat is scraped from the outside of the skull, a chisel can be used to open the palate in the roof of the mouth so that the brains can also be removed.

There are two other access points that must be opened. The large "ball-joint" at the base of the skull must be carefully chiseled out, and the sinus passage up through the nose must also be cleared. Other small passages containing nerve endings should be picked as clean as possible with wire or some other suitable instrument.

When the skull is completely clean of all meat and tissue, both inside and out, it should be polished to a bleach-white with cleanser on a wet cloth. Later, after the skull is completely dried, it can be shellacked and mounted on a board. A satin finish can be obtained after it is shellacked by applying a light amount of pumice before waxing the skull.

The process of caring for hides and skulls is tedious and time consuming. But it is the final chore of Brown Bear hunting, and the last step in an overall operation that guides like Pinnell and Talifson spend most of each year just gearing up for. Because hunters often spend a total of ten to fifteen thousand dollars on their hunts, there is every reason to do the best possible job caring for their trophies.

CHAPTER V

There was a sense of relief around the Olga Bay camp after the hides and skulls were cared for. Rain had fallen for several days while the crew finished their tasks. But just as they concluded those operations, the wind shifted to the northwest, bringing clear skies, sunshine and much warmer weather. I immediately became eager to hit the trail and explore more of Brown Bear territory.

A local bush pilot reported to P & T that he had seen a small herd of reindeer in the Ayakulik flats just north of Red Lake. Although reindeer were only of indirect interest to me at the time, I knew that hungry spring Browns sometimes prey on them. Bears also can be spotted grubbing for various plants and vegetables in the same area. So, I decided to pack up and head for Red Lake. I left Olga Bay the very next moring.

The center of Red Lake is about eight miles north of Olga Bay. P & T have a cabin at the lake's north end. Many call this location the best Brown Bear territory on the island, and it is, at times. In the fall, Red Lake is full of salmon. Bear hunting is good at that time. The Ayakulik River, which drains the lake, is one of the best salmon spawning streams in Alaska. The big fish swarm into the lake each summer, and scores of brown bruins gather around its shores to dine on them. In the fall, P & T often glass right from the cabin. Many large Browns are shot within a short distance from camp. Also, the Ayakulik River meanders through the expansive Ayakulik flats, draining thousands of potholes and smaller streams which extend almost 20 miles to the northwest. A great number of salmon spawn throughout the flats and attract bears during the fall. But Red Lake is notoriously poor hunting in the early spring season because few bears den there in the winter. However, after the bruins leave their dens and begin to rut, they seem to spread out over most areas of the island, including those adjacent to Red Lake, in search of food and each other. So I expected to see my share of Brown Bears.

Between Olga Bay and Red Lake lies Akalura Lake. Akalura is a large T-shaped body of water approximately four miles long in both directions. The east-west portion is to the south and is about a mile wide. The north-south section is about half as wide. Akalura is quite deep. The beaches along its south side are narrow or non-existent, and most of the shoreline is choked with heavy growths of willow and alder.

Akalura Creek flows out of the lake's south side, dropping approximately 40 feet to the high-water mark of Olga Bay. The stream is about 35 feet wide and 3 feet deep at the outlet; it flows several knots per hour until reaching rapids less than a quarter mile from the lake where the current accelerates greatly. The creek's bed is chiefly gravel and shingle, but heavy stones and small boulders along its course create much turbulence. In places the stream banks are high cut and the water swift. In others, further downstream, the creek meanders through grassy flats. This is perfect Brown Bear habitat.

About a quarter mile upstream from the cannery, the Alaska Department of Fish and Game (ADF&G) maintains a cabin which is used in the summer by biologists who count salmon as they pass through a weir on their way to Akalura Lake. The bears appreciate the biologists and frequently try to assist them in counting fish. Understandably, when the big bruins show up to help count, the biologists back off and let the bears do *all* of the work.

I began my trek to Red Lake by following the narrow boardwalk that is maintained between the Olga Bay cannery and the ADF&G camp. About half-way between the two locations, however, I took a side trail to the north. This trail generally runs parellel with the creek until the latter jogs back to the east and northeast; it took me to the west end of Akalura, where I had a clear shot around the shore of the lake's extreme north end. The weather was beautiful for cross-country hiking; the fresh, clean air was slightly scented with the smell of early growth.

Near Akalura, the trail curved westerly, up along the side of a tall ridge separating the lake from the territory to the south. This ridge, which consists of glacial deposits, extends the entire width of the valley below Akalura Lake. In fact, it forms a natural dam which retains the lake, except at the lake's outlet where Akalura Creek flows through a gap in the great wall.

Scientists say that almost all of Kodiak Island was covered with ice at one time. This writer believes that most of the northland was covered with ice after waters from a great flood receded. That ice has slowly melted, and has left lakes behind. If one observes, it is obvious that the entire topography of Kodiak resulted from excessive amounts of water seeking outlets to the sea. The earliest lakes became swampy flats after those outlets were found and most of the water drained into the sea. When these changes transpired, streams on the island shifted, were cut in half, and in some cases reversed their flows. Even Olga Bay once was a fresh-water lake. It was created by an ice dam; when the ice melted, salt water entered from the southeast.

Looking east from the west end of Akalura, I saw the rough, jagged pass into Fraser Lake country. Huge rock outcrops characterize the center of the pass. A steep, narrow trail can be followed up through the outcrops. Just looking at the scene made me appreciate the conveniece of the path I trod. For years, P & T made annual snowshoe treks over the Fraser pass with their hunters. The guides packed all of the camp gear, their personal gear, and all of the hunters' gear as well; they sometimes spent entire days struggling to cross it. On one occasion, six men spent several days hauling a heavy plywood skiff over the pass to Fraser. It's a natural passage, but a terribly rugged one.

Traveling around the west side of Akalura seemed easier than my earlier trip from Larsen's Bay to Karluk Lake, in spite of the fact that the trail was scanty to non-existent. My muscles were becoming properly toned by heavy backpacking, and the aches I felt after my first day afield no longer troubled me. My pack was somewhat lighter now, too. I had left some non-essentials at the cannery.

A few clouds were passing overhead as I neared the north end of Akalura. The lake became shallow and the water much warmer near the head of the lake, a perfect spot for mosquitoes bent upon eating me alive. Fortunately, higher altitudes beyond the lake's north end would eliminate some of the critters. The Ayakulik portage rapidly rises from Akalura's north end at an angle of about 50 degrees, before leveling off into a large flat area for the remaining mile and one-half to Red Lake and the rest of the Ayakulik watershed.

Like the long glacial deposit that provides a dam for Akalura, the portage area between the two lakes is also a great glacial deposit. But this natural dam features one of the most unusual natural wonders to be found on Kodiak Island: possibly the oldest bear trail in the world. Four feet deep in places, this ancient trail is filled with ample evidence of the huge behemoths that constructed it. Judging by the tracks exhibited there, the trail is a regular Brown Bear freeway. There's no telling how many centuries have lapsed since the first bruin began working on it. I considered the trail's great depth as I navigated its narrow passages, being fully aware that I was trespassing on the personal property of Mr. Bear.

No one knows when the first Brown Bear arrived on Kodiak Island. One thing that scholars do agree on, however, is that the big bears were among the first creatures to call the place home after its ice mantle receded. Only five, and possibly six, species of land mammals are native to Kodiak. These are: Brown Bear, Red Fox, Otter, Northern Vole, Ermine and possibly Ground Squirrel. The latter species may have been the first successfully transplanted mammal on the island, because there is historical evidence that it was intro-duced from North Simidi Island by Koniag natives who prized its skin for making parkas, etc.

All things considered, however, the Brown Bear probably was the first inhabitant of the island. Red Fox and Ermine require smaller prey for survival, and only one species, the Northern Vole, could have filled that need. Some scientists believe that the Northern Vole was the last of the native species to arrive from the mainland. Because Otters would be less capable of survival than Brown Bears, before fish populations became significant in the lakes, a small population of Brown Bears must have originally relied upon the earliest vegetation on Kodiak for sustenance. The bears hibernate during the winter, so they were able to survive on summer vegetable growth. Later, after fish became abundant, Otters began migrating to the area. After birds moved in, Ermine and Red Foxes followed, dining on the feathered creatures, as well as Northern Voles, whenever the latter happened to arrive. Thus, Brown Bears probably were the first to inhabit Kodiak Island after the ice receded. As I walked through the narrow, four-foot-deep passages of the great bear trail over the Ayakulik portage, I was awe-stricken by the Brown Bears' permanence.

Red Lake is typical of the large lakes on Kodiak Island. Like Karluk and Fraser lakes, Red Lake originally encompassed a larger area to the north, which now constitutes swampy flats and riverbeds. But as the sea-ice receded around the island, an outlet was formed at the present mouth of the Ayakulik River, allowing most of the water to drain. Now, dammed behind the large glacial deposit between it and Akalura Lake, Red Lake drains into the Ayakulik at its north end. Except for its shape, Red Lake is very similar to Akalura, in just about every respect.

I was forced to walk on slippery rocks in the water for much of the distance around Red Lake's shores, because of choked and clogged alders that obstruct land trails. I almost fell on the moss-covered rocks several times. P & T and their clients often have walked around Red Lake to their hunting camp at its north end. More than one of their hunters have fallen on these rocks, sometimes knocking rifle scopes and parts of their own bodies out of alignment.

I arrived at Red Lake camp shortly after eight p.m., thoroughly exhausted and ready for a good night of rest. Soon, three plump, freshly caught Dolly Varden trout were sizzling over the cabin stove, to the accompaniment of a crackling fire. Life couldn't have been better!

CHAPTER VI

All of the fair weather had vanished by morning. A cold, 40-knot southwest wind was bringing in heavy rain from the North Pacific. Gusts of wind were shaking the small P & T cabin, and I was happy to be indoors. Clearly, the island was in for a big storm.

If I would be weathered in for several days, I wanted to enjoy as varied a menu as possible. So I scouted the camp pantry. Not only did I find pancake mix and several cans of processed meat, but I located a selection of jams and peanut butter. I wouldn't starve!

Due to the cool weather, I became concerned about the amount of wood that I was burning from Morris Talifson's private stock. So, I also located a nice bow-saw in the back room and decided to replenish his woodpile before departing. Alder is the only burnable firewood at Red Lake, and one has to walk at least a quarter-mile from camp to find any.

In spite of the storm, several trout in the Ayakulik were feisty enough to swallow my "golf-tee" lure. One of these was over 18 inches long. It was a rainbow and was surprisingly fat. I cleaned two of the smaller fish and laid them out for dinner.

That afternoon, I decided to go ahead with the wood cutting. There were several large clumps of alders near the lakeshore which had good-sized limbs. These soon were reduced to four-foot lengths, lashed to my packboard and carried to camp. The work day was shortened by a heavy overcast. By five o'clock, I was content to retire to the taste of my trout, sizzled to a golden brown.

Kodiak Island has a unique flavor all its own during big storms. The heavy cloud cover, coupled with tumultuous wind and cloud movement, causes humans who are confined within that environment to feel a closeness that is difficult to describe. While the weather rages with immeasurable violence only short distance above the ground, even the lower level 40-knot winds feel mild by comparison. Yet, the wind at the lower elevation is violent enough to raise treacherous waves on lakes and bays, and to cause even the strongest of characters to seek refuge in camp.

I recall several storms that I endured while trapping on Kodiak during my very first Alaska winter. There were several places on my trapline where the wind was funneled between mountains, in such a way that its velocity was greatly increased. So strong was this wind current, that I was forced to lean at a great angle in order to walk against it. Several times I tried turning my back on the wind and jumping, to see how far I could be blown. The wind pushed me almost three feet.

On several occasions the wind was terrific at higher elevations, and sounded like the roar that comes from a busy freeway in the city, or several loud freight trains rolling across a big bridge simultaneously. The clouds in the sky moved at such speeds that I guessed that the wind must have been blowing at over 200 knots at 1,500 feet elevation. However, on the ground where I walked, the wind was just a slight breeze. I never forgot that a giant was passing overhead, however, and this fact made me feel puny by comparison.

No doubt my experiences had a lot to do with my love for Kodiak Island. Kodiak is alive with adventure. Yet the land remains surprisingly forgiving to those who master its characteristics. Give me Kodiak Island and the rest of the world can have all that is called "civilization."

Although "civilization" has affected even Kodiak, not many winters have passed, in reality, since the island was as wild as wild can be, and was inhabited only by the big bears and a very proud group of Natives.

No one knows when the first Natives arrived on Kodiak Island.

And no one knows for sure if the Natives now on the island were the first. They simply were on the island when the first Russians landed, and had developed a respectable relationship with the big bruins.

The proper name for these Kodiak Natives is "Koniag." Although they are often confused with the Aleuts, who live to the southwest in the Aleutian Islands, they are of Eskimo stock. They spring from the group of Eskimos originally called "Kaniagmute."

The Konaigs utilized Brown Bears for food, clothing, fuel, and even shelter. Although the beasts were one among many species harvested, they could, and sometimes did, provide all of the Konaigs' necessities. But in spite of this close relationship with the bear, the Koniags feared the animal, and maintained many superstitions regarding it.

The Koniags believed that the Brown Bear was part human, part animal, and part spirit. They believed that the beast could transform itself into a human simply by eating a human. Conversely, the Koniags also thought that they could transform themselves — into bears — by chewing on the face skin of a bruin, and stretching this skin until it covered their entire bodies.

In the minds of Koniags, bear atrocities were sometimes linked to family feuds and adulterous situations. One myth had it that a woman committed adultery with a bear. After her "bear lover" was killed by hunters, the vengeful woman chewed the bear's face skin and became a bear. She then attacked her own family and villagers to avenge the death of her lover.

A similar story involved a deserted wife who became a bear and killed her husband and his second wife, as well as her own children.

Another story was that a bear, in human form, entered a village and carried away one of its men. The captive pretended to be dead while being carried to the bear's den. But, upon entering the den, the bear's cubs began choosing which parts of the man they would eat. So, to avoid being eaten, the man cast a spell upon himself, which made the animals lose their desire to eat him.

The most fascinating legend probably is the one involving a "white-faced" Brown Bear. White-faced brownies sometimes occur on Kodiak. The Koniags told of a group of men in a village who were jealous of the best bear hunter around. To get even, these jealous individuals persuaded the local Shaman, or witch doctor, to transform the great hunter into a bear. When the hunter was transformed into a bear, he had a white face. Later, as it turned out, this white-faced bear somehow was retransformed into a human. He then felt so sorry for the bears that he killed a fellow bear hunter who refused to stop killing them.

On one of Morris Talifson's hunts, the guide watched — and protected — a white-faced bear before his hunter downed a very nice trophy in the same locale. Perhaps the Koniags would say that Talifson's success was attributable to the mercy he showed this unusual bruin.

Despite their shamanistic rituals relating to bear-human transformations, the Koniags often hunted bears, and the animals played a key role in other aspects of their beliefs. The Koniags believed that bear hides could be used as good luck charms. Koniag women commonly remained prostrate for days, covered only with bear hides, in the belief that this influenced certain spirits to aid their men who were hunting whales.

Koniags employed several weapons against the big bears. Sometimes they built huge traps, consisting of many sharp spikes that were so arranged that the bear could be forced to walk over them. The spikes pierced the bear's feet and crippled it, so that a group of Koniags could easily overtake and slay the animal with spears. These spears had poisoned slate heads on them.

Koniags were sometimes even more sophisticated, especially when warring with other Natives. They actually developed personal armor made of thin sheets of slate, which is very abundant on the island. Later when the Russians landed, such armor even proved semi-effective against the whites' crude musketry at longer distances. But due to its weight, slate armor probably was a real handicap in any kind of close combat.

Before the Russian era began, Koniags used an assortment of weapons and implements for general hunting and fishing activities. They used dip nets and spears for salmon in the rivers. They also constructed weirs, or rock fish traps, in shallow streams to guide the fish to their nets and spears. On the open sea they used hooks and lines for cod or flat fish. Back on shore, other Koniags constructed huge nets of seaweed or whale gut; they set these for birds, capturing whole flocks of Ptarmigan and ducks. These nets were used for salmon fishing, too.

Koniags were fond of bear meat. There were no herds of beef, Reindeer, or Black-tail deer on the island in those days. So the Brown Bear was the only large land animal within their territory.

One early Russian explorer reported that the Native crew of his six-man "bidarka" (a large skin boat) devoured an entire, full-grown Brown Bear in only six hours. However, this writer questions whether the explorer exaggerated his point. Nevertheless, another account states that a similar crew ate two 50-pound Halibut in just eight hours. So, perhaps these crews were starved at sea before falling upon their delectable steaks.

After killing a Brown Bear, especially in the late fall when the animals had been feeding on berries, Koniags emptied the bear's stomach and entrails of their contents before boiling the organs with fresh berries. Some Russian explorers reported these dishes with less than favorable recommendations.

As in the case of seals, Sea Lions, and Sea Otters, Koniags also used bear entrails for making raincoats, or waterproof parkas. After the entrails were removed and emptied of their contents, they were turned inside out so that all fatty particles could be removed with sharp pieces of shell, etc. Then the entrails were repeatedly washed in salt water or urine, before being hung to dry. After becoming dry, the entrails were cut into long strips and softened underfoot or by hand rubbing. Once soft, these were fashioned into waterproof garments called "kamleikas." Brown Bear kamleikas were considered the most durable.

In the fall, Brown Bears are extremely fat. The Koniags utilized this fat for cooking purposes, and also for burning in their stone oil lamps.

Brown Bear hides, of course, were used for many purposes. The Koniags made tents from them. They also made warm coats called "parkees" from the big skins. These were their warmest coats. The Koniags put no hoods on their parkees, but had small openings at the necks that were just large enough for their heads to pass through. Koniags also used seals, Sea Lions, Sea Otters and Ground Squirrels for this same purpose. They even used feathered skins from Cormorants and other waterfowl.

Although the Brown Bear played a dynamic part in Koniag culture, the Koniag way of life was structured around the ocean and its vast cache of resources. Most of the Koniags' hunting was done at sea in "kaiaks" or "bidars." The kaiaks consisted of a slight frame of light wood, tied together with whale sinews, and entirely covered with seal skin, with the exception of hatches for the oarsmen. These boats were made with one, two or three hatches. Each hatch was covered with a waterproof apron, which could be drawn tightly about the oarsman's armpits in bad weather. This kept the rest of his body dry, and prevented disaster in the event of an upset.

Besides kaiaks, the Koniags used a much larger boat called a "bidar." Bidars were open on top and much heavier than kaiaks. They were used principally for long journeys, and some could carry 30 to 40 persons. In addition to oars, masts and sails often were used to propel bidars.

From these boats the Koniags hunted sea mammals, and in season fished for salmon. The sea mammals provided skins for boats, coats, and tents, and meat and oil for human consumption. The hunters were accustomed to traveling far from shore — and were not at all afraid of rowing 20 miles out into the open ocean.

Koniag whalers often approached to within 20 to 30 feet of great whales before throwing their spears. Usually one man in the front hatch of a kaiak would do all of the "shooting." The "shootist" would aim for the center of the whale's back. As soon as the weapon was thrown, the other hunter would paddle away from the whale as fast as possible. A wounded whale could destroy their boat and cause their deaths if the Koniags failed to get out of its way.

Wounded whales die slowly, but the Konaigs were patient and waited several days for the dead mammal to wash ashore. Although hunters sometimes lost their whales, the mammals usually were recovered by parties from other villages farther up the coast. If a whale had been afloat for some time, the Natives tested the meal by watching gulls. If the birds wouldn't touch it, then they wouldn't either.

Koniags hunted sea otters by surrounding an otter with 12 to 15 kaiaks before attacking it. Once wounded, the otter would dive and try to escape, but each time the wounded otter would come up for air, another 12 to 15 kaiaks would be waiting to form a new circle.

Finally exhausted, the sea otter would fall prey to the hunters. As many as 100 kaiaks would participate in such a hunt.

Salmon provided the Koniags' most important means of subsistence. Each year the Koniags dried tons of salmon and stored the fish inside their houses — stacked like cord wood. In a good year, entire floors would be covered with several feet of dried salmon; families actually lived on top of their food supply, gradually eating their way to the floor.

Regardless of what type of meat was eaten, be it whale, seal, fish, or Brown Bear, Koniags almost always dipped it into some kind of oil before eating it. The Koniags seemingly valued few commodities as much as they valued oil. The Brown Bear provided its share of oil for Native use, but Brown Bear fat probably was used mostly for fuel.

According to the first Russians to arrive, Koniags were accustomed to going barefooted. Some authorities say that the climate on Kodiak was much milder in those days, so perhaps there is truth to this report. In any event, the Russians claimed that the Koniags quickly adopted the "torbassá" boot brought from Siberia. These were made of seal or deer skin.

The traditional Koniag house was the "barabara," which was a sod hut. The Koniags usually excavated the floor areas so that it was several feet deep. The dirt and sod that were removed were used for walls and roofs as soon as stout frames were constructed from driftwood. Barabaras had doors in their sides which were skin covered; there were small holes in the center of each roof so that smoke and sunlight could pass through. The latter openings had removable covers made of stretched sea mammal bladders. These barabaras apparently were *not* bear proof.

In 1741, the first Russian expedition sailed within range of Kodiak Island, but it didn't stop there. The Bering expedition suffered greatly from various disasters before returning to Siberia with great numbers of sea otter pelts, some of which were taken near Kodiak. During the next two decades, most Russian activities were confined to the Aleutian Island. But in September 1763, Stephen Glotov dropped anchor in a sheltered bay somewhere on Kodiak's south end.

Glotov's first encounter with the Koniags was an unfriendly one. The Natives maintained a safe distance from the Russian vessel, and an Aleut interpreter could not understand their tongue. Not surprisingly, when the Russians actually landed, they found the Natives' village deserted. A few days later a small party of Koniags approached with an Aleut slave, and the first dialogue between Russian and Koniag cultures began.

The Russians didn't ask much of the Koniags. They insisted that the Natives recognize and pay tribute to the Czar, and that they provide hostages (to secure future payments in sea otter pelts). Needless to say, this traditional form of Russian "peace" plan was rejected.

A few days later, the Koniags attacked, formally demonstrating their own attitude toward detente with the Russians. A large number of Koniags sneaked up on the strange boat and showered it with arrows. When the Russians answered with muskets, the Koniags fled, leaving behind an assortment of incendiary devices. This incident convinced the Russians that the Koniags were far more intelligent and warlike than the Aleuts. When the Koniags returned four days later, they carried various wooden shields in an apparent attempt to deal with Russian lead. When these failed they immediately contrived other protective devices, including traditional slate armor.

Finally, three weeks later, the Koniags began building portable breastworks. Between 30 and 40 warriors concealed themselves behind each of seven such structures and began their advance on the Russian ship at low tide when it was helplessly aground. Soon the ship was under seige and being peppered with a hail of spears and arrows. The only choice that the Russians had was to mount a swift charge against the bulwarks. This ploy worked. The Natives didn't expect such a bold counter-attack; they became frightened and fled. After this battle, the exasperated Natives disappeared.

At least one account of an original encounter between Russians and Koniags, from the Koniag point of view, has survived the passage of time. In the 1800s, an old man named Arsenti Aminak recounted incidents he remembered from his childhood.

"I was a boy of nine or ten years, for I was already set to paddle in a bidarka, when the first Russian ship with two masts appeared near Cape [Trinidad]. Before that time we had never seen a ship; we had dealings with the Aglegnutes of the Alaska peninsula, with the Tnaianas of the Kenai peninsula, and with the Koloshes; and some wise men even knew of the Californias; but ships and white men we did not know at all. When we espied the ship at a distance we thought

Olga Bay cannery during the early 1940's. Photo courtesy of P & T collection.

Bill Pinnell mans the Karluk River wier—one of Alaska's longest—while working for U.S. Fish and Wildlife during the late 1930's. Photo courtesy of P & T collection.

Morris Talifson, left, shows off part of his season's catch during the early 1940's. Photo courtesy of P & T collection.

Bill Bignell harvests his garden crops at Bight. (Photo courtesy of E. F. Elliot.)

Bounty from the seas—King Crabs and prawns. Photo courtesy of P & T collection.

Bill Pinnell's trapping barabara in the Ayakulik Flats. Photo courtesy of P & T

There's no shortage of cranberries on Kodiak. Photo courtesy of P & T collection.

They got "two-bits" for each claw. Bounties were paid on Bald Eagles until federal protection was extended. Photo courtesy of P & T collection.

Fish-traps made salmon canning very profitable. Photo courtesy of P & T collection.

Bill Pinnell and two friends show off their catch—two King Salmon and one Sockeye Salmon. Once landed, the big Kings must be wrestled and killed. They can withstand most clubbings, and usually must have their backbones severed. Photo courtesy of P & T collection.

Agents of Alitak Reindeer Company with a reindeer ready for the butcher-block. The first 62 reindeer were planted on Kodiak in 1921; the herd hasn't been tended since the 1940's, and now numbers about 500 head. Photo courtesy of P & T collection.

Bill Pinnell with eleven-foot Brown Bear hide. Photo courtesy of P & T collection.

Another remarkable trophy taken by one of Talifson's hunters. Photo courtesy of P & T collection.

Bill Pinnell and his crew went gold mining on Kodiak's south end in 1970. They stayed in this cabin (since collapsed).

They labored hard.

Bill Pinnell manned the hand-watered sluice box.

And showed a young packer how to pan concentrates.

After several days, the men had recovered enough gold for each person to have a nice sample.

it was an immense whale, and were curious to have a better look at it. We went out to sea in our bidarkas, but soon discovered that it was no whale, but another unknown monster of which we were afraid, and the smell of which made us sick. The people on the ship had buttons on their clothes, and at first we thought they must be cuttlefish, but when we saw them put fire into their mouth and blow out smoke we knew they must be devils, as we did not know tobacco then. The ship sailed by the island of Aiakhtalik, one of the Goose Islands at the south end of Kodiak, where a large village was situated, and then passed by the Cape [Trinidad] into [Alitak] Bay, where it anchored and lowered the boats. We followed full of fear and at the same time curious to see what would become of the strange apparition, but we did not dare to approach the ship. Among our people there was a brave warrior named Ishinik, who was so bold that he feared nothing in the world; he undertook to visit the ship and came back with presents in his hand, a red shirt, an Aleut hood, and some glass beads. He said there was nothing to fear, 'they only wish to buy our sea otter skins and to give us glass beads and other riches for them.' We did not fully believe his statement. The old and wise people held a council in Kashima, and some said: 'Who knows what sickness they may bring us; let us await them on the shore, then if they give us a good price for our skins we can do business afterward.'

"Our people formerly were at war with the Fox Island people, whom we called Tayaoot. My father once made a raid upon Unalaska and brought back among other booty a little girl left by her fleeing parents. As a prisoner taken in war she was our slave, but my father treated her like a daughter, and brought her up with his other children. We called her Plioo, which means ashes, because she had been taken from the ashes of her house. On the Russian ship which came from Unalaska there were many Aleuts and among them the father of our slave. He came to my father's house, and when he saw that his daughter was not kept like a slave but was well cared for, he told him confidently, out of gratitude, that the Russians would take the sea-otter skins without payment if they could. This warning saved my father, who, not fully believing the Aleut, acted cautiously. The Russians came ashore together with the Aleuts and the latter persuaded our people to trade, saying, 'Why are you afraid of the Russians? Look at us, we live with them and they do us no harm.' Our people, dazzled by the sight of such quantities of goods, left their weapons on the bidar and went to the Russians with their sea-otter skins. While they

97

were busy trading, the Aleuts, who carried arms concealed about them, at a signal from the Russians fell upon our people, killing about thirty and taking away their sea-otter skins. A few men had cautiously watched the result of the first intercourse from a distance, among them my father. These men attempted to escape in their bidarkas, but were overtaken by the Aleuts and killed. My father alone was saved by the father of his slave, who gave him his bidarka when my father's own had been pierced with arrows and was sinking. In this bidarka he fled to Akhiok. My father's name was Penashigak. The time of the arrival of this ship was the month of August, as the whales were coming into the bays and the berries were ripe. The Russians remained for the winter, but could not find sufficient food at [Alitak] Bay. They were compelled to leave the ship in charge of a few watchmen and moved into a bay opposite Aiakhtalik Island. Here was a lake full of herring and a kind of smelt. They lived in tents here through the winter. The brave Ishinik, who first dared to visit the ship, was liked by the Russians and acted as a mediator. When the fish decreased in the lake during the winter the Russians moved about from village to village. Whenever we saw a boat coming at a distance we fled to the hills, and when we returned no [dried fish] could be found in the houses. In the lake near the Russian camp there was a poisonous kind of starfish; we knew it very well, but said nothing about it to the Russians. We never ate them, and even the gulls would not touch them; many Russians died from eating them. But we injured them also in other ways. They put up fox traps and we removed them for the sake of obtaining the iron material. When the Russians had examined our coast they left our island during the following year.''

Modern-day Koniags claim that their forefathers withdrew to Olga Bay whenever the Russians approached. Olga Bay is accessible by boat only through the Olga Bay Narrows, which resembles a large river from the outside. The Koniags claim that the first Russians never discovered Olga Bay and that it remained a place of refuge for some time — not only for themselves, but also the Brown Bear.

In any event, Kodiak Island never was the same after the Russians landed. A new, more awesome character had interjected himself into the country where Koniags and Brown Bears previously had lived undisturbed. From that time onward, the Brown Bears faced far more than the spears, arrows, and spike traps of the Koniags. In fact, the beasts' former tormentors soon became the tormented. Instead of being one of the many species relied upon by the Natives, the Brown Bear was destined to become a sought-after prize in its own right. The old ways continued for almost 20 years after Glotov's band of marauders departed Koniag territory. But in 1784, Grigor Ivan Shellikov, a man with greater ambitions, landed on the island and brought about permanent change. Within two more years, the once proud and brave Koniags were hammered into subjection by that Russian. Thereafter, the old ways of the Koniags began to vanish. Change had come to stay, and Kodiak still is changing — even today.

CHAPTER VII

I waited at the Red Lake cabin two more days while the raging North Pacific storm howled. Four-foot waves crashed into the shore with rhythmic regularity. How the P & T cabin remained standing will remain a mystery to me.

In spite of the weather, I continued catching Ayakulik River trout for most meals. I love fresh trout fried to a golden brown. These fish were fat — the kind that most fishermen yearn to catch. They weren't "stocked" trout, but were native to the Ayakulik and its many tributaries. Life was terrific!

Fish have always figured highly in the diets of Kodiak residents. In the old days, Koniags depended heavily upon salmon. They had no calendars, but predicted with incredible accuracy exactly what species of salmon would be ascending each stream at any given time. Depending upon the purpose for which the fish were intended, the Koniags moved about from stream to stream, acquiring desired stocks.

Just north of the Olga Bay cannery, is the site of an original Koniag fish camp. There is an old barabara there; its remains are barely visible beneath heavy growth of elderberry bushes. When I worked for P & T, I frequently stopped at the barabara site and viewed the remains of the old stone weir that the Koniags built just east of it. The Vshaped outline still is visible although many stones have been washed downstream.

Akalura had fantastic runs of salmon in the days when ancient Koniags guarded their weir with spears and dip-nets. Dried fish, or "ukala" as it was called in the Native tongue, was the mainstay of their winter diet, and was the basis for much barter. In fact, the first Russians probably would have starved to death except for the dried salmon they stole from the Natives. Now, the Koniags no longer live along Akalura Creek, and the salmon runs there are not so bountiful.

The ancient Koniag culture was virtually destroyed by the time the United States purchased Alaska in 1867. The people still were dependent upon the land for sustenance, but their dependence had shifted so that the Koniags' economy was based upon trade and commerce rather than pure subsistence.

Before the Russians arrived, the Koniags obtained every necessity of life directly from the land or sea. But because the Russians forbade Koniags to wear clothing made from Sea Otters, Brown Bears and other valuable furbearers, they were forced to hunt these species for purposes of trade with the Russians. The Russians sold the people cheap cloth parkas, in exchange for fortunes in pelts. In addition, the Koniags became dependent upon European food staples, tools, and other implements. The more dependent the Koniags became, the less valuable their fine resources became in terms of trade. Russians have always been willing to take advantage of the weak.

By the time Alaska became American territory, many of Kodiak's resources were severely depleted. Conservation of Sea Otters was practiced during the latter years of Russian rule, but their numbers still did not reflect their former abundance. Brown Bear and other furbearers were depleted, too, but the historical details regarding the same are not as graphic as in the case of Sea Otters.

Unfortunately, the one major Kodiak resource that managed to escape serious depletion under the Russians was only destined to become the most exploited resource under American rule. Salmon still darkened the waters around Kodiak when the first Americans arrived. And wealthy San Francisco entreprenuers were quick to seize this opportunity.

During the Russian era, a large-scale salmon-salting operation had existed at the mouth of the Karluk River. In those days, as many as 10-14 million salmon ascended the Karluk to spawn each year. According to one reputable report, during at least one season, salmon were so plentiful at the mouth of the Karluk that a boat could not be pulled across the stream. The Russians only salted a few hundred barrels of Karluk salmon each year. But by 1896, American salmon canneries at Karluk packed 1,650,000 red salmon (sockeye) annually, not to mention other species.

The first salmon cannery on Kodiak was built on the Karluk Spit in 1882. Four more canneries were operating in that vicinity within seven more years, as well as others located elsewhere around the island.

In 1889, Arctic Packing Company built the first cannery on Olga Bay. It was located at what is now known locally as the "Upper Station." Although the two Upper Station lakes enjoyed fabulous salmon runs in those days, the operation was unsuccessful due to poor equipment. Consequently, new equipment was shipped in, and the cannery was moved to a more convenient site across the bay. "Cannery Cove" became the home of the "Olga Bay cannery," and the bright red buildings that were erected there remain to this very day. A few years later the cannery changed hands, and has since been owned by the Alaska Packers' Association.

Olga Bay flourished in those days. It was a population center of some significance. Consequently, the location is rich in colorful history which rivals that of the wild west days in the "Lower 48." Although most of the stories were buried with the passage of time, Bill Pinnell still recalls the tales he heard when he arrived in 1938.

"The winter watchman and cannery superintendent were around here for years and had pretty good recollections of things that went on here years before, as well as the stories they'd heard from older hands," Pinnell explains. "There also was an old diary that belonged to the superintendent, but it got stolen by one of our hunters years ago.

"In the old days, the cannery was like a small town. There were over 20 buildings here, in addition to a number of cabins and barabaras. The little building that we use as our headquarters was the dispensary, but the winter watchman lived in it during the off season. We have our kitchen and radio room in it now, as well as a couple of beds. The big cast-iron stove in the kitchen has been there since the cannery was built, so it's close to 100 years old. It burned coal when we got here; coal became hard to get so Morris converted it to oil.

"Alaska Packers used to employ a lot of Chinese labor, but later they brought in the Filipinos. The Chinese came over on contracts: a Chinese person would contract with the company to provide so many workers for the cannery.

"He'd tell his fellow Chinese, 'If you'll go to Alaska and work for me for so much — after you're in America for so many years — you can became a naturalized American citizen.'

"Well, that's what the Chinese wanted. They didn't care a hoot about the job! They wanted to become American citizens. So the Chinese labor master would contract his workers out to the cannery for dirt-cheap wages. They were just like slaves working for the head Chinese. After they had been here for awhile, they could go down to San Francisco to Chinatown, or elsewhere in the U.S., and do as they pleased! The Chinese weren't so dumb. They just wanted to become American citizens. They'd heard about the 'land of plenty.' And considering the way they had to live in China, you can't blame them for wanting to come over here for a better life.

"Well, then they brought in the Filipinos, and things got rough and heavy around here for awhile. The Filipinos and Chinese hated each other, and the company had an awful time keeping them from fighting. There were three Filipino brothers killed here in one day by the Chinese, and they're buried up there on the hill behind the warehouses. They had a line drawn down the center of the dock; one side was for the Filipinos, and the other for the Chinese. The Chinese would get all doped up on opium and the Filipinos had hot tempers. The U.S. marshal from Kodiak came down and arrested as many as 16 men at one time.

"Several years after we got here, Morris and I were looking around in one of the buildings they used to call 'the morgue.' One of the cannery superintendents told us that he'd seen as many as 11 Chinese and Filipinos in there at one time — after a big fight.

"Out in what used to be the cookhouse, or mess hall, there still are signs of a shoot-out. Just inside the door was a big steel-topped table that the cooks worked on. There still is an indentation on the metal where one bullet hit and ricocheted into the wall. The Chinese cooks were working in there when a filipino stuck a gun through the door and killed one with a bullet through the head. Then the other cook ran outside with a sawed-off shotgun and killed the Filipino as he tried to run away. Oh, it was really something around here for awhile when the Chinese and Filipinos were at each other's throats!

"Of course, time marches on, and a lot of the things that happened here are lost to dust and decay. The old cookhouse — where the Filipino shot the cook and got shot in turn — it fell down years ago. There's nothing left of the cookhouse except the stove and steel-topped table, a few chairs and old bottles. But that's the way all things end, when you think about it."

Pinnell isn't the only oldtimer who remembers the cannery the way it used to be. An elderly Koniag gentleman says that when he was a very young man, he worked at the Olga Bay cannery for only ten cents an hour. This old man was born in a barabara not far from the cannery, and his grandparents experienced Russian domination. He vividly recalls cannery life during the old days.

"One day a big bear came up to the cannery and sat down in front of the door of the retort building. No one could get through that door and we had to use one on the other side of the building." He says today, "It didn't hurt anyone — just sat there looking at us. Several days later, the superintendent finally killed the bear."

According to some reports, whenever the cannery needed fish, a huge seine was hauled out from the end of the dock, around in front of Akalura Creek, and was pulled in with tens of thousands of salmon in a single haul. There also were fish traps along the beach inside Olga Bay which supplied fish for the cannery. By the time P & T arrived, most of the salmon were exhausted, and the Olga Bay cannery had shut down.

"Although the salmon were wiped out," Pinnell explains, "the unions caused the cannery to shut down. All of the freight into Olga Bay had to be reloaded onto a smaller boat at Trap Point so it could be brought through the Olga Bay Narrows. When the longshoremen at Moser Bay and Trap Point went union during the depression, Alaska Packers couldn't afford to run the Olga Bay cannery. The union asked for too much money, so instead of having lower-paying jobs, the workers wound up with *no jobs* at all.

"Morris and I had a similar experience with unions down south during the depression. We wanted to work — to stay alive — and couldn't, because we weren't members of *their* union. So, we have pretty good ideas as to what unions are all about!"

Although unions put an end to the cannery business in Olga Bay, the other local industry — gold mining — suffered a different sort of fate. Several years before P & T arrived on Kodiak, as many as 35 gold miners sifted black sand along the southwest beaches of the island. Today, only a few of their shacks remain. Pinnell tells why.

"There were two miners who lived together, bought their food together, but had separate claims," he says. "One of these was an old German fellow, and the other was a real young man. Well, one day the young fellow got too close to the old German's claim. So when the young man came in that evening, the old German met him at the door and shot him in the chest with a shotgun.

"The other miners put the young man in a dory — he wasn't dead yet — and rowed to Karluk Village where there was a wireless station. The young fellow died before they got him to a doctor, however.

"Then, the U.S. marshal came down and arrested the German and took him back to town. When the trial came up, all of the miners were also rounded up for witnesses. The nearest court in those days was at Seward or Valdez, and by the time the trial was over, the miners had missed their season. Most of them never came back. They went elsewhere, where the mining was better."

In spite of the modest prospects, Kodiak looked pretty good to two hungry miners during the Great Depression.

"We had fish, rabbits, and reindeer to eat, and the weather wasn't too cold much of the year. Besides this, we could make wages from mining," Pinnell explains.

P & T were used to working 12 to 16 hours daily and thought little about moving several cubic yards of overburden in order to reach a few colors.

"We did real well one year when we got good winds with the right tides," says Pinnell. "But most of the years we only made enough to get by on. That's why when the cannery watchmen's jobs opened up for us, we never went back to the beach as miners."

Most of the beach is laden with heavy, large gravel, several feet deep. The fine gold dust beneath this overburden has been collecting for milleniums. The glacial moraine deposits above the beach contain extremely small amounts of gold. As these bluffs are eroded by tidal action, the gold collects just beneath them in the wash. So the better collections of gold on the beaches are spotty, and their locations depend entirely upon the day-to-day winds and tides.

"Sometimes we'd dig down four feet and not find a thing," says Pinnell. "But we could come back to the same location after the next tide, and there would be quite a bit of gold there. Some days we worked all day for 10 or 15 cents. But once in awhile, we'd hit the tide right and really clean up. Those were the days we always worked towards.

"Today," he adds, "mining is practically impossible. After the 1964 earthquake, the earth sank. As a result, a lot of gold is now out of reach below tide. Also, with the Refuge being in place, you can't build cabins like you used to be able to. The natives don't seem to want anyone to make use of their land either. So, as a practical matter, mining is all washed up on Kodiak."

CHAPTER VIII

After beseiging me at Red Lake cabin for three days, the howling North Pacific storm relented, and fairer weather returned with a northwest wind. On that fourth morning, I enjoyed a steaming stack of hotcakes and hot coffee before beginning activities north of camp. I planned to hike toward a long spur that juts out into the flats from the east about three and one-half miles northwest of Red Lake. From there I would command an overpowering view of the flats.

The stream flowing from Red Lake is only one branch of the Ayakulik. The Ayakulik has its head almost 14 miles northwest of its juncture with the Red Lake fork. However, because of its connection with Red Lake, the Ayakulik is known locally as "Red River." The real Red River is much smaller and flows into the ocean north of the Ayakulik. All zigs and zags considered, the Ayakulik is about 40 miles long, and gathers water from at least 32 significant tributaries.

As mentioned earlier, all of the Ayakulik area was at one time a large lake. When the great ice caps retreated, most of the water drained into the sea. Left behind were thousands of small lakes and potholes, and a very thick (40 to 70 feet) layer of wet, mucky moraine (mud). Most of this territory is now covered with moss, grass and sedge-covered tussocks ranging in size from a few inches to four feet tall.

Although poorly drained, the ground usually supports at least some form of stunted plant life. But there are areas where nothing but a very thin layer of bright green moss grows, over what could best be described as watery mud or muck. The ground near these places usually supports some growth, which covers two or three inches of "soil." Then, beneath that small amount of soil is an abyss of black, jelly-like moraine that has all of the characteristics of quicksand. Hikers usually suffer great difficulties out in the flats during warm weather when the ground is not frozen solid. Although one naturally tries to skirt these areas, they cannot all be avoided. If a hiker is fortunate, he will feel the qround quiver like jello and can change his route. But, if forced to continue, he probably will break into the muck sooner or later.

Pinnell tells of one unfortunate hunter who was almost swallowed by one of these sinkholes.

"We'd gone along quite a ways," he says, "when I noticed that the hunter was missing. I told my assistant to go back up the trail to find him. When my assistant found him, the hunter was in up to his neck and was hanging onto willows for all he was worth. Why he hadn't hollered, I'll never know, but the assistant said his face was *red as a beet!* We worked for quite awhile pulling him out. We almost lost both of his hip boots but fished them out by running our arms down into the muck after he was pulled free."

Local lore has it that humans have died in the Ayakulik flats as a result of these sinkholes. In any event, walking over and about sinkholes is at least very tiring and troublesome. The constant ground quiver keeps a person off balance and makes him feel as if he were walking on a waterbed. Until the ground freezes solid very late in the fall, the Ayakulik flats area is not hospitable for bear hunters, who would be well advised to hunt more favorable terrain elsewhere on the island.

Near camp, the Ayakulik seemed devoid of wildlife. Green growth was just beginning to sprout in some places. But the stream was full of fat Dolly Varden trout that were waiting to devour salmon eggs as soon as the bigger fish arrived. Magpies also were abundant; these darted from bush to bush ahead of me, scolding loudly. A strong breeze felt zesty against my face. I savored the odors of spring that it carried.

Less than a mile downstream, I discovered several places where

110

bears had been digging for roots. Brown Bears rely heavily on vegetable growth in the spring and early summer. In addition to a large assortment of roots, they eat grasses, sedges, tubers, etc. They also consume a variety of other vegetables and plants such as wild parsnips, skunk cabbage and shriveled berries left over from the year before. The rooted spots that I found were within a few score yards of each other, some distance above the river, near a big patch of willows. Each was a few feet wide and a couple of feet deep. I couldn't determine what kind of roots had been dug, but the bear left plenty of seven-inch tracks behind — indicating that it was an eight-footer. I glassed for awhile, then continued downstream.

Shortly thereafter, I realized that I was in the vicinity of the place where I saw bear diggings of a different sort during my very first season as an employee of P & T. Those diggings were the beds of a very large boar. The old boy had made them above the river during a cold snap; he had rooted about digging clods of sod and grass until comfortable hollows were constructed in the ground.

P & T teach their young guides that usually only boars will uproot wads of sod. Such beds usually indicate the nearby presence of possible trophies. Sows, on the other hand, tend to bed in grass without grubbing too much. Some bears build their beds near convenient fishing holes, and retire to them for naps between salmon snacks. Others position their beds on top of prominent points where they can survey adjacent terrain for intruders.

Many bears are shot while they are sleeping in their beds. This may sound unsportsmankile, but I've never seen a sleeping bear remain asleep after a changed wind blows human scent its way. The bears are *always* on guard. So what difference does it make what the beast is doing when it's killed?

I turned from the river and began hiking north toward an over-looking mountain. At this point, well-drained alder and grass were giving way to the real flats, such as those described earlier. I was about two miles downstream, near a small pond that P & T affectionately call the "mudhole." This little lake harbors salmon in season. Being so close to camp, it provides convenient hunting when northwest winds prevail. The brush is not too thick there, and bears that are fishing near the little lake can be easily spotted.

An added attraction at the mudhole is excellent Ptarmigan gunning

111

during the fall. On bright days, after light snowfall, Ptarmigan seem to be everywhere in the area. There is no better upland bird shooting on Kodiak as far as this writer is concerned.

Near the base of the mountain, I was surprised to discover the work of newcomers to the area. Although transplanted to the north end of Kodiak decades ago, Beavers began reaching the south end only ten years ago. Now, Beavers are in the Ayakulik flats, and a family of them had dammed a small streamlet near the mudhole. The dam obviously would block salmon, but it surely added a new feature to the countryside.

Another recent newcomer to Kodiak's south end is the Blacktail deer. Again, these animals were rare on the south end of Kodiak ten years ago. During my first winter, one buck passed through Akalura country north of Olga Bay. It apparently was exploring in advance of does that were to follow. Several years passed before I actually saw a Blacktail on the south end; I saw it while bear hunting at Karluk Lake.

The Blacktail herd on Kodiak has received much attention lately. Biologists are quick to use it as an example of a successful big game transplant. One game manager told me that as many as 10,000 deer are harvested on Kodiak annually. Most of these are taken on the north end, however, where hunters can fly minutes from town and bag three or four in a single day.

This sort of hunting is an opportunity for modern-day sportsmen to enjoy the kind of gunning experienced by their grandfathers. Although the bag limit has been as high as seven deer per season, it was reduced to five in order to thin out hunters — not because the deer were being overhunted. Many of the deer taken in recent years have had exceptional racks, and some have weighed over 200 pounds field-dressed; so the Kodiak experience is a quality trophy and meat hunt.

In order to successfully hunt Kodiak deer, the hunter must recognize that the animals change their habits and haunts with the seasons and weather. During the summer, deer are high above bears, giving birth to young and eating browse near mountain tops. As winter approaches, the animals move to lower elevations. When severe weather hits, they find shelter on south slopes, and sometimes feed on the beaches if snow is deep.

Some words of caution are in order for prospective Kodiak deer hunters. Bears have become wise to the fact that easy meals are available after deer are shot. They'll come into camps looking for meat, especially late in the season after the salmon have been eaten. Therefore, hunters should hunt with rifles big enough to kill bears. Meat should be hung in a location away from tents or cabins, where it can be watched from a distance. This prevents the hunter from being surprised by a bear just outside the door.

Like Interior grizzlies, Kodiaks are very protective of kills that they have claimed. Several deer hunters have been mauled by the animals in recent years. Most deer hunters who use their heads avoid problems with bears. But ADF&G is becoming increasingly concerned about the others who don't use their heads and wind up killing bears "in defense of life and property." A bear is worth more than a deer, they say; therefore, hunters should simply let the bears have their deers once the big beasts lay claim to them. This is probably very sound advice in most cases.

After leaving the Ayakulik, I didn't stop climbing until I reached the highest ridge beneath a summit overlooking the flats. Clouds were beginning to roll in from the Shelikof Straits further north, and I also spied rain squalls approaching. Hopefully, my vantage point would help me spot bears, and perhaps Reindeer.

There is no closed season and no limit for Reindeer hunting on Kodiak. ADF&G officials classify the animal as "Caribou." However, the animals really are descendants of reindeer that were owned by the Alitak Reindeer Company back in the 1920's. Although this herd has had ups and downs, it has been at low ebb for decades. However the reason for the herd's decline was not hunting. A disastrous fire destroyed much of its range years ago. And P & T still tell of it.

"The story was that several men set fire to their cabin while they were drinking," Pinnell explains. "The fire spread, and our sky was black with smoke for days. The remaining range soon was overgrazed, and the herd never fully recovered."

The Natives originally owned the Reindeer, but their interest in animal husbandry was choked by their love for the sea. Today, the Reindeer are wild for all practical purposes. The Natives haven't tended them for decades. Yet, some of the oldtimers in the villages still feel that they have a legitimate claim to the animals, and resent

113

ADF&G classifying them as "Caribou."

Originally, the Bureau of Indian Affairs managed the Reindeer harvest, which was not restricted to Natives. In those days, the nearest government official often was the village school teacher, who was authorized to issue Reindeer harvest permits.

It so happened that one year Pinnell bought a harvest permit for only one Reindeer. Later, he came upon a small band of Reindeer at the head of Olga Bay; He immediatley decided to "fill his tag" because these were so close to home. He still tells of the incident.

"I drew a bead on a nice fat Reindeer and shot," he explains. "The Reindeer didn't go down, and they all ran over a low hill. Pretty soon, the running Reindeer re-appeared, and as they went over a second hill I shot again. Still no luck. Finally, the animals went over a third little hill, and when I shot, the Reindeer went down.

"Well fine. I started over to get my Reindeer, but as I crested the first hill, I found that the first Reindeer I had fired at was dead after all. Now I had two Reindeer — one more than I had harvest permits. I felt bad, but, I slit the animal's throat, gutted it, and went for the second one. However, when I crossed the second little hill, there was the second deer I had shot at. It was dead, too. I had killed *three* Reindeer and only had *one* harvest permit. Now I really felt bad.

"Well, there were some Natives nearby, and they came over to see what the shooting was about. When they saw I had shot three Reindeer, they took off for the village. They went to the school teacher and told him that 'Pinnell was killing *all* the Reindeer!'

"When I finally got things under control, and had the meat taken care of, I decided I had better go to the village (Akiok) to talk to the school teacher, and see if I could explain. Fortunately, the school teacher was very kind to me and simply made me buy two more permits. That was that. I had three Reindeer, and no one ever came after Bill Pinnell for 'killing *all* the Reindeer.'"

For years, P & T relied upon Reindeer for their meat supply. After the two began guiding, they also featured the animals as game trophies. Some of their hunters took exceptional heads, too. One of Pinnell's favorite tales involves a Reindeer hunt.

"The hunter already had his bear," Bill recalls, "but he wanted a Reindeer. So I took him down Bare Creek looking for them. There was no bag limit on the animals, but we only allowed our hunters to take three head.

"Well, we found 30 or 40 head grazing below 'Green Point.' I was gonna look them over, but he didn't give me a chance; he just started shooting and didn't stop until three were dead. When we got up to the downed animals, the hunter scratched his head and wondered *how in the world* he could have killed three cows out of a herd that size. I didn't have the heart to tell him that there wasn't a bull in the whole herd! But it sure was funny watching him scratch his head over that one."

By the time this writer arrived on Kodiak in the early 1970's, Reindeer on the south end were scarce. Although I heard regular reports on their whereabouts, the herd usually grazed in places such as Gurney Bay, Grant Lagoon and the Ayakulik flats.

I continued glassing the Ayakulik flats, but finally headed for camp late in the afternoon. Several light showers dampened my view, but the day basically was a good one for glassing. I spotted several foxes near the Ayakulik, and a fair-sized bear crossing the flats further north. I didn't see any Blacktail deer or Reindeer.

CHAPTER IX

The day after my hike north of camp, a southwest wind returned, and I was obliged to look for game in a different direction. Accordingly, I set up my spotting scope just outside the cabin and began scanning the distant slopes of mountains to the southeast. This area seemed promising, so I decided to pack up and head for it.

Connecticut Creek empties into Red Lake about a mile southeast of the P & T cabin. Its valley is broad and flat, but toward the south, the ground slopes gently upward into a large canyon with a back door that opens into Fraser country. To the north, the land rises abruptly under the shadow of steep mountain walls and a smaller but lofty canyon recess. Other than scattered stands of red willow, the bottom of this valley is covered with head-high grass during the later summer months. The new growth of green grass had barely begun to show at this early date, and the country still was covered with a thick mat of crushed brown straw from the previous season.

Although I expected to be rewarded with the sight of several Browns before the day ended, I was surprised to spot a medium-sized bruin so early in the morning. It was about midway up on the slope south of Connecticut Creek. From its appearance, the animal was simply passing through. It had just come from Fraser Lake country, via the canyon to the south, and was moving around the mountain at a pretty good speed.

The bear looked like it might be a young boar. It was about an eight-footer and was rubbed baldly on the side that was visible to me. As previously mentioned, a great number of Kodiaks are rubbed in the spring. The percentage of rubbed bears taken in April and early May ranges from 33 to 50 percent each year, as opposed to only 9 percent for those Kodiaks taken in the fall. Spring rubs tend to be far worse than fall rubs, too. In fact, Kodiak guides sometimes refer to these badly rubbed spring bears as "poodle dog bears."

Rubs are caused in a variety of ways. Sometimes during the winter, moisture forms between a bear's fur and the side of its den and freezes. When the animal rolls over, its guard hair is pulled loose or broken off where it is frozen fast.

Rubs also are caused when a beast rubs against rocks in the den. When a bear begins traveling in the early spring, rubs usually appear on the backs of its paws, due to the hair rubbing against hard-crusted snow each time it takes a step.

A different sort of rub — but not a "rub" in the truest sense of the word — is caused by the bear's natural shedding process each spring. These rubs are easy to spot because they give bears such a pathetic appearance. When shedding takes place, the underfur becomes terribly matted and clings to the beasts in big shaggy globs. These are the rubs that most often cause guides to speak of "poodle dog bears." The animals look like recklessly sheared poodles until all of the globs of matted fur have dropped from their hides sometime later in the summer. By that time, the bears have uniform coats of short, new fur. This short coat of fine fur then grows constantly; by mid-October, the beasts are fully furred again, and are ready for the rigors of another winter in the sub-arctic.

Only very old and sick bears that are not meant to survive another winter usually fail to grow full coats of fur in the fall. However, such animals are rare in country that is regularly hunted. As for healthy bears, a small amount of fur growth continues during the winter while body functions are slowed by hibernation. This extra growth accounts for the extra fur that makes *unrubbed* spring hides a little more desirable.

Another point to remember regarding rubs, is that during the spring hunting season they're usually found on the rumps and backs of bears, where the fur normally would be longest or thickest. Fall rubs often are restricted to the flank areas where bears rub against brush while

118

traveling cross-country. Fall rubs usually are less noticeable than spring rubs and thus are easier for the taxidermist to conceal.

Fall hides have another advantage over spring hides. Like other fur-bearing mammals (such as the "cherry-red" fall season red fox), bears have their finest-colored fur early in the season. Fall hides usually are darker and have richer color tones — often dark chocolate brown. After eating oily salmon all summer, fall season Kodiaks have fur that glistens with a peculiar sheen. When bears come out in the spring, their fur may be somewhat longer, but it often is dull and drained of vitality. Spring hides bleach quickly while their owners soak up long hours of warm sunshine reflected off of hard-crusted snow.

All of this is not to say that spring hunts are not worthwhile. An *unrubbed* spring hide is a beautiful trophy. Spring hunters do enjoy advantages such as longer daylight hours and a higher percentage of large boars killed. So, each hunter must decide which hunt he prefers.

As just indicated, large boars usually are the first to appear in the spring. Younger boars and sows, particularly sows with cubs, are slower to leave their dens. Some of these big bruins sit by their dens for days, while others begin traveling right away. The animals that sit by their dens can be difficult to spot from the ground, but the big bears that begin moving cross-county really stand out, especially against snow. The beasts which decide to travel can be seen plowing through deep snow — up and down steep mountains — just like bull dozers. Later, after the snow melts, the animals are less obvious, but clearly visible, just like the bruin I watched moving above Connecticut Creek.

I watched the beast skirt the valley. It slowly lumbered along with large wads of matted, shedding fur dangling from its rump. This animal would have made a poor trophy; the fine coat of dark, lustrous fur it probably wore six months earlier now was ugly and bleached by long hours of spring sunshine. When the bear neared Red Lake, it turned south and headed toward the big trail over the Ayakulik portage.

I left the cabin shortly before nine a.m. and hiked along the Red Lake beach toward Connecticut Creek. A lone Bald Eagle soared high overhead while I climbed, seemingly unconcerned that I aspired

119

to reach its altitude. After rounding the mountain for half a mile, I found a sheltered spot and began glassing for bears.

Like the rest of Red Lake country, Connecticut Creek is not prime territory during the spring bear hunting season. It is a good location later in the summer when it becomes a major thoroughfare for Browns. Probably every bear on Kodiak's south end uses the valley from time to time. It is the most convenient route between all three of the island's principal lakes and the massive Ayakulik flats. Because the bears were in full rut, I believed that there would be traffic to observe.

As I stood overlooking the valley, I could see Connecticut Creek winding back and forth across the canyon floor, laced with innumerable bear trails. Five miles east, I knew that the headwaters of another stream drained toward Fraser Lake. Almost 20 miles northeast flowed the Karluk River. Finally, if human eyes could see so far, one would be able to view Larsen's Bay, almost 30 miles distant in the same direction.

Few humans in recent times have walked long distances on Kodiak. The island's mountainous backbone and swampy lowlands are too rugged for extensive hiking. In the old days, Natives sometimes crossed the island by foot despite the fact that they spent most of their time at sea hunting seals and whales. They ventured inland to hunt or hide from enemies. When they did this, they usually stayed high on mountainsides where brush is sparse and where big bears are less of a threat.

One "modern" foot traveler who still is remembered by Kodiak oldtimers was "Walking Pete." "Walking Pete" was from Montana and was a third-generation mountainman — the son of a Shawnee Indian squaw. P & T still talk about this character.

"He showed up at the cannery when we first moved here," Talifson recalls. "He wore nothing but little ol' short pants and a pair of moccasins in warm weather. In the winter he wore wool shirts and pants. The guy walked all over the island and would stay out in the hills for months without being seen by human eyes. He had two shepherd-type dogs and packed enough food for them and himself. If he caught a fish — that was extra. Most people thought he was crazy. He finally disappeared with his dogs, and nobody ever figured out what happened to him. We always figured that a bear got him."

P & T also did a lot of walking during their early years on the island. They didn't own a boat, so Pinnell usually hiked down the beach 40 miles to Alitak for the mail and supplies.

While I relaxed between two great grass tussocks, I scanned the slope opposite Connecticut Creek for bears. An hour passed, then two. Finally I ate lunch. When the afternoon was well under way, I began thinking that my vigil was in vain. But shortly before three o'clock, I spied what I had been waiting to see.

Near the head of Connecticut Creek, a small blond sow with three cubs of the year was coming my way. The older bear stopped periodically and pawed for edibles; occasionally she looked over her shoulder at her cubs. The little bruins seemed inseparable as they bounced over and around tussocks. They obviously were enjoying their first year of life.

Although female Kodiaks often go into heat and attempt to breed as early as their third year of life, they seldom conceive until their fourth or fifth year. Then, they may continue conceiving every third year for most of the rest of their lives. No one really knows the maximum age at which sows can conceive. Doubtless it varies from sow to sow, but probably is less than 20 years. Sows as old as 16 years of age have been known to give birth. I couldn't determine the age of the animal I observed, but she didn't look like a really old animal.

The Kodiak breeding season lasts for about ten or twelve weeks. The bears usually begin rutting by mid-May and sometimes continue until August. During the rut, Browns are extremely ruthless, difficult to stalk and very dangerous when successfully approached. Boars are naturally protective of their sows; if they hear a noise, they may rush headlong toward whatever made it. P & T have been charged on a few occasions under such circumstances.

Brown Bear cubs are born while the sows are hibernating, between January and March, after a gestation period of approximately 265 days. Litters range in size from one to five cubs. Litters of two or three cubs are most common. At birth, the cubs have no hair or teeth, are entirely helpless, and weigh less than a pound each. But they begin growing fast, even before they emerge with their mothers in the spring. By spring they weigh from six to fifteen pounds. And by the end of their first summer season young Kodiaks can weigh as much as 175 pounds. This is a phenomenal growth rate, but it doesn't end there. Even though cubs may lose 25 percent of their weight during

121

their first winter of hibernation, they regain all of the lost weight, and may weigh over 300 pounds after their second summer season.

Sows with cubs are rather social creatures. Sows have been observed visiting other sows while their cubs romp together. Sometimes these visits last for several days. Some observers claim to have seen sows split with the wrong cubs, even taking almost all of another sow's cubs when these visits terminate. This is very likely because cubs sometimes nurse the wrong moms while the sows are visiting.

Anyone who watches Kodiak cubs for long soon learns that they are full of antics. The two cubs I observed certainly were clowns. One cub enjoyed climbing tussocks and hopping off onto the backs of its siblings. It did this several times before the others reacted physically. When their mother noticed the scuffle, she turned and gave two of them a good bounce.

Unfortunately, cubs don't always play close to their mother. When they become separated, they pose great hazard for unwary hikers who blunder between them and the sow. Bear maulings occur each year. Often the offending sow only reacts to a perceived threat to her cubs. Hikers should always avoid walking between sows and cubs when traveling in bear country.

The cubs were eager to rest when mom decided to relax. As soon as she sat back against the hillside, all three youngsters took advantage of her position and nursed. Then, to my left, I noticed more movement near the mouth of the canyon on the north side of Connecticut Creek. Another bear, a big one, was moving out into the valley.

This bear's frame was massive. Its body was much longer than it was tall; it had a big round dishpan face and a good-sized snout. The bear's ears and eyes appeared tiny in relation to the rest of its head, which in turn looked quite small relative to the rest of the bruin's body. Finally, the animal simply dwarfed the red willows it walked through. The beast's big hump was accentuated by the fact that much of its fur elsewhere was badly rubbed, leaving its shoulders covered with long, fluffy fur.

But for the hide's condition, this Brown would have made a wonderful trophy. The bear surely would measure at least ten feet square, so it almost had to be a boar. Meanwhile, the sow and cubs remained where they were, unaware of this big bear's presence. The wind still blew from the southwest, and I wondered what the female's reaction would be if she ever winded the other's scent.

As the big Brown moved farther across Connecticut Creek valley, the probability that the sow would smell it became apparent. Finally, when the boar was in the mouth of the opposing canyon, the sow smelled him. Her reaction was swift. Just as soon as the male's scent apparently reached her, she hoisted herself aloft on hind feet and began waving her nose back and forth, sniffing the air. The sow obviously was alarmed. Then, almost before her startled cubs regained their balance, she lowered herself to all fours and wheeled about to flee. The sow certainly wanted to avoid the boar, because she hustled her cubs toward the head of Connecticut Creek as fast as they could move.

I have seen sows with cubs run from boars on a number of occasions. Once while hunting near Karluk Lake I observed a sow with cubs fishing in a small feeder stream. Suddenly, the trio became alarmed and began running back the way they had just come, glancing over their shoulders periodically. This behavior puzzled me until I spotted a big boar approaching. The sow and cubs clearly were avoiding that big bruin, too.

Brown Bear boars, especially the big ones, are notorious cub killers. Many times, there isn't much that an average-size sow can do to protect her cubs from such a big animal if it decides to make a meal of one — or two — of them. Bill Pinnell says that he did see a sow successfully defend her cubs on one occasion, however.

"I never actually saw a boar fight a sow over a cub," he says, "but. . .one time a bear rolled rocks down the hill and it looked like it was just deliberately trying to hit one of the cubs. He missed the cubs and accidentally hit the sow. And boy, when he hit her with that rock, she went up that hill after him. The last we seen of him — he started to cross a gully that had a big snow slide in it, and his feet went out from under him, and down that gully he went head over heel."

Pinnell tells how this sow defended her cubs, but cubs aren't always so fortunate. Anyone who spends much time in bear country sooner or later finds bear excrement full of cub fur. The fine, sometimes white, bear-hair rope that passes from killer boars is clear evidence of infanticide.

Some observers have even reported catching boars in the very act of eating cubs. One Alaskan reported seeing a boar eating a cub while its mother and sibling watched nervously from afar. Another report has it that a boar attacked a sow and cubs, separating the cubs from their mother. The sow apparently never rounded up all of her cubs after the attack, and some time later a dead cub was found. It had been killed by a much larger bear.

Alaska Brown Bears are not the only bears in North America that have cub-killing tendencies. Studies elsewhere in Alaska, Canada and lower United States have proven that infanticide is common and widespread among ordinary Grizzlies and even Black Bears. In fact, in some states where Black Bear populations were meager for years, game officials discovered that more liberal seasons actually resulted in overall bear population increases. Hunters bagged big boars, so more cubs survived.

Several theories have been advanced to account for infanticide among bears. One is that boars kill cubs in order to thin out future competition. This may be true in whole or in part. However, I hold to the theory that big boars kill cubs so their mothers will be forced back into heat sooner. This is supported by the fact that only one-third of the sows are available for breeding during the rut, whereas all healthy boars are available. There is fierce competition among grown boars for all available sows, and young cubs standing in the way can easily get killed. Studies of similar patterns in populations of lions, tigers, and baboons have concluded that this is a likely cause of infanticide among those animals. I believe that it is just as likely to be true among bears.

Although infanticide probably is by far the biggest cause of cub mortality, cubs die from other causes too. Common diseases such as distemper have been cited. Accidents also take their toll. Cubs have been know to starve to death after accidentally becoming separated from their mothers. Sows occasionally abandon their cubs before they are able to care for themselves, too.

The normal mortality rate among cubs from all causes combined is enormous. Studies have shown that as many as 40 percent of all Brown Bear cubs may perish before the end of their second year. Consider the fact that sows normally only breed every third year, and it's easy to understand just how vulnerable Brown Bear populations are. If the killing of sows and cubs were not restricted, and if a large percentage of single sows were killed by hunters, the population could be gutted for years.

I appreciated the benefits of sound bear management while watching nature unfold before me. The frightened sow and cubs soon disappeared, and the big boar apparently never knew that the other animals were nearby. Soon, it too disappeared in the distant mountain passage.

With a little luck, the sow's cubs would survive to maturity. If they would survive to the end of their second summer season, or the beginning of their third, the sow finally would drive them into independence, thereby protecting them from amorous males. But, I decided that I'd probably never know whether these cubs would survive so long, and quietly headed back to Red Lake cabin beneath a setting sun.

CHAPTER X

I had spent five days at Red Lake, but there was more Brown Bear territory to be explored. I yearned to visit the "outside" beach at the mouth of Ayakulik River. Even though the first salmon would not appear in fresh water for several weeks, I'd seen several bears that were moving toward salt water — an indication that the fish season was on the way. So, maybe there would be more Browns further downstream. A new northwest wind also promised fairer weather for enjoyable hiking.

I "buttoned up" the P & T cabin while morning freshness still prevailed and silently departed. A short distance down-river, the Ayakulik is shallow enough to cross with little difficulty. A bear trail begins there too, on the west side of the river near two little lakes. This trail winds up into a pass before dropping into the lower Ayakulik flats. The route is a real shortcut and saves several miles of tramping. I took it with the intention of heading straight down the river toward salt water after reaching the Ayakulik.

At the top of the pass, I rested my pack on a tussock and sat down to absorb scenery. An opposing mountain shielded several small feeder streams from view, but I could see all the way up the flats to Grant Lagoon, almost 20 miles to the northwest. I was astonished by this scene during my first season as a packer for P & T. Then, the flats seemed so awesome, beautiful, and empty. Experience soon taught me that they also are very rugged.

Descending from the pass, I kept a sharp eye for game. There were no Reindeer in sight, and no bears either. A Bald Eagle soared overhead to remind me that I wasn't alone in the country. Other creatures also were on the move. Several Magpies scolded loudly at my advance.

Out in the flats, I immediately encountered huge, three-foot sedge-covered tussocks that were studded with scraggly, stunted red willows. These were the same tussocks that tested my mettle when I packed my first *big* bear hide as a packer. I'll never forget that hide. It weighed 127 pounds without the skull, and almost broke my back. The pack I now carried weighed over 75 pounds and quickly became burdensome as I "hopscotched" from tussock to tussock.

When still some distance from the Ayakulik, I glanced toward the northwest and happened to notice movement on the horizon. It was a lone bruin tredding across the flats toward a canyon to the west. A tributary of the Ayakulik flows from that canyon, which probably also contained fine beds of vegetables that Browns rely upon before salmon arrive. When the animal was out of sight I continued toward the Ayakulik, where I finally stopped for lunch.

While eating lunch, I was surprised to encounter yet another of the island's carnivorous residents. It was a rather intelligent-looking Red Fox that was sitting on a nearby tussock watching me as I downed cups of hot soup and tea.

"You're looking for a hand-out!" I scolded the furry creature.

The fox didn't budge. It seemed unworried that I might be dangerous. This kind of behavior is typical of foxes in isolated parts of Alaska.

Excepting the Weasel, the Kodiak Red Fox probably is the island's most abundant furbearer. The Kodiak Red Fox is unique in that it is one of the world's largest and is generally considered to be a genuine subspecies of the ordinary Red Fox. Even though the Kodiak Red lacks the fine fur that is worn by Reds in Alaska's interior, it is very heavily furred and thus is excellent for coat-making purposes. During times of high fur prices, the Kodiak Red is actively pursued by a corps of local trappers. One such period had just ended when P & T arrived at the Olga Bay cannery, and Pinnell explains how the Kodiak Reds were affected by it.

"When we first began trapping around the cannery," he says, "there weren't many furbearers around. The Natives had been trap-

Near world's record bear killed by Morris Talifison in 1949. The skin measured more than eleven feet square. Photo courtesy of P. & T collection.

These three bear hides and hunters appeared in the P & T ad for over 25 years. The spring hides were not "square skinned"; note the large rub on the tail end of the left

Eleven-foot Kodiak taken by Bill Pinnell while trapping. Photo courtesy of P & T collection.

Taking time out on the trail. Photo courtesy of P & T collection.

Eleven-foot bear taken by Morris Talifson. Photo courtesy of P & T collection.

Beautiful ten-footer taken on an early spring hunt. Photo courtesy of P & T

Smallest Brown Bear ever taken on a P & T hunt. The hunter was advised of its small size, but had a special use for the small hide. Photo courtesy of P & T collection.

Bill Pinnell stands on a ladder above the hunter and his trophy. This man spent over a month hunting for a big bear, and scored a ten-foot November trophy. Photo courtesy of P & T collection.

Another fine November Brown Bear hide and proud hunter. Photo courtesy of P & T collection.

Another fine November Brown Bear hide and proud hunter. Photo courtesy of P & T collection.

Ten-foot brownie bagged by a young Canadian.

P & T hunters come from every direction, and from every walk of life. These two never will forget stalking this beast. Photo courtesy of P & T collection.

This huge, old boar had been in many fights during its lifetime, and had a scarred nose to prove it. Photo courtesy of P & T collection.

This ten-foot Kodiak was taken by one of Talifson's hunters. Photo courtesy of P & T collection.

This bear hunter took time out for fly casting. Photo courtesy of P & T collection.

Kodiak also has the world's finest Steelhead streams. Photo courtesy of P & T collection.

The front paw of a ten-foot six-inch Brown Bear. Note the white claws which are indicative of age.

The hind paw of a ten-foot six-inch Brown Bear.

ping them heavily in that area several years before. We found dozens of rusty traps that were left behind. They were scattered all over the country. Some of them even had bones left in them. So we decided not to trap anything between the cannery and Akalura on the west side of the creek. After three or four years there were foxes everywhere, and they soon began hanging around the cannery where we fed them. Some even became quite tame.

"Of course, we were fur farmers back in Montana," Pinnell continues, "so our first inclination was to live-trap Silvers and Crosses (color phases of Red Fox) and cage them until we were through trapping Reds. We figured that by caging as many of those valuable color phases as possible, the overall fox population would show a high percentage of them. But over a many-year period, this idea failed to produce any more Silvers or Crosses.

"We had several Silvers that almost became members of our 'family.' And if they got caught in our traps accidentally, we would bring them back to the cannery and cage them. Only once or twice did any of these get badly hurt in traps and have to be destroyed."

By and large, Kodiak foxes are among the smartest anywhere. They usually are so well fed by spawned-out salmon and other seafood combed from beaches during the winter, that they exhibit little interest in bait. In fact, they are difficult to catch with any kind of bait until January when these natural foods are less plentiful. So trappers often use snares and traps along trails where the foxes travel.

During my own first Alaska winter, I witnessed starvation among Kodiak foxes. In December of that year, an extremely long period of deep cold and snow began and lasted until May. Six feet of snow blanketed the highlands, and four feet of ice covered fresh-water lakes. Even the salt water of Olga Bay was tightly gripped by two feet of ice, permitting ski-plane landings at the cannery until May. Salmon had been scarce that year, and foxes were completely cut off from seafoods usually combed along the shores. The foxes were forced into the hills to hunt ptarmigan and rabbits. Because the animals usually are well-fed beachcombers, they lacked the hunting skills that were needed that year. By February, I found a fox on the beach, so weak from starvation that it couldn't walk. Even during this period, many of the foxes were extremely cautious at traps and proved difficult to catch.

There was one trap-wise Red that I particularly remember. I had a "cubby" set under the roots of a wind-blown alder near the mouth of Akalura Lake. A single number-four double-long-spring trap guarded the cubby in which I'd placed part of a fox carcass for bait. A rather wise fox uncovered my trap, then went to the rear of the cubby, dug through several inches of dirt, and squeezed between roots. The fox stole my bait and made me look foolish.

On my next visit I discovered this situation and decided to rebait the set. This time I placed a second trap — a number-three jump trap — just inside the hole that the fox had squeezed through. I was sure that the unsuspecting canine wouldn't discover the new trap before it would get caught. But the fox did discover the trap. To demonstrate its superior intelligence, the fox returned to the front of the cubby, overturned my first trap, and stole my bait again.

Finally, I placed the entire skinned carcass of an otter in the rear of the cubby and set both traps right on top of it. Then, I hauled several armloads of grass from a nearby windswept slope and completely filled the cubby. On my next visit, the old, grey-muzzled red was madly tangled in both traps.

Morris Talifson remembers a similar incident involving a Silver fox that actually left a pile of excrement right on top of his trap.

"When the fox did that," he says, "I knew I had a smarty on my hands. But I eventually caught it.

"I was checking my traps up near the lake," Talifson continues, "and had just gone over a little rise when my dog stopped and began 'pointing' up the trail toward the same set. When I looked, I spotted this fox digging out one of my traps again. So, I put a stop to its mischief real quick."

Kodiak foxes maintain a close relationship with Brown Bears. As soon as the bears are catching large numbers of salmon during the summer, foxes frequent the same streams and pick up scraps that are left behind. If fishing is very productive, Browns will eat only the belly section of each fish, and sometimes not even that much. The bears have the habit of squeezing salmon under paw to see if they contain eggs. If a fish is loaded with eggs, the belly is quickly bitten out and the rest is dropped. If the salmon is a male, and has no eggs, it may only be killed before the bear loses interest in it. So,

Kodiak foxes grow extremely fat devouring these salmon each year. In fact, Talifson says that some of the foxes he has caught after good salmon seasons have weighed almost 40 pounds. A 40-pound fox is a *big* fox. Talifson also says that some of those jumbo foxes died in his traps as a result of apparent heart attacks; this probably resulted from over-exertion. The foxes simply were too fat to endure the stress.

The Ayakulik River Red Fox apparently had no fear of me and would have been an easy mark for a trapper. I watched the animal and later followed it about taking close-up pictures of it. Finally, I shouldered my pack and continued toward the mouth of the Ayakulik and the "outside" beach.

There were a number of bear tracks along the lower stretches of the Ayakulik, but these were scarce enough to convince me that Browns hadn't yet "homed" in on the salmon stream. So, the big animals still were devouring vegetables, roots, and the remainder of last season's berry crop.

Understanding the seasonal movements of Brown Bears is important for successful hunters. As stated earlier, the older boars usually are first to emerge each spring. Therefore, early spring hunters have an excellent chance to down large trophies before the smaller bears emerge. The situation is completely reversed, however, in the fall; understanding bear movements during the intervening months helps explain why.

Before salmon appear, Kodiak Browns remain in constant flux, moving from high to low ground, and vice versa, in search of food. These erratic movements are encouraged by the rutting season, but the biggest boars may remain in more isolated locations until the arrival of salmon. When salmon runs hit hard, Kodiaks concentrate near streams where they eat fish and continue breeding.

During the fishing season, most bears spend their time moving up and down streams, fishing and sleeping at intervals. When fishing, bruins usually walk along streams or lakeshores, often sideways — facing the water — until a fish is spotted. Then, in an instant, the beast charges into the water so fast that the fish is unable to escape before being pinned beneath the bear's paws. Almost always the salmon is pulled from the water in the bear's mouth. The big bears may never swat fish ashore with their paws the way some artists have fancied them doing; although this method is possible for an animal the size of a Brown Bear.

Throughout the fishing season, sows, especially those with cubs, maintain home ranges of less than ten miles' radius. Boars move about more freely with ranges of at least 25 miles' radius. Big boars sometimes travel 50 miles in a single day, fishing at several locations along the way.

In August, as the rutting and fishing seasons wind down, a new crop of berries ripens on higher ground, and Kodiaks begin moving back and forth between fishing holes and berry patches. Also, the bigger boars drift back toward their secluded haunts, where their daytime activities diminish. They can later be seen cleaning up the last of the remaining salmon in small streamlets and potholes wherever these may be found.

By the middle of November, most of the smaller single bears and sows with cubs have headed for their dens. But the big boars remain afoot as long as there are salmon to be found, or until hard winter weather encourages them to "turn in" for the winter. This usually occurs by the first week in December.

Only occasionally do bears refuse to enter their dens after hard weather hits. More often, if a bear is restless during hibernation it will only arise and step outside for a breath of fresh air. Sometimes a restless bear can be seen walking outside its den, but seldom will it go far. A few bruins will simply lie out on an open slope all winter, half awake, and never really hibernate — especially in mild winters.

Some Kodiaks hibernate in the same den year after year. Talifson has observed this. He once watched a sow come out of the same den every spring for half a dozen years. He became quite fond of her. One year, however, she had no cubs and was mistaken for a boar. Talifson regrets that he allowed his hunter to shoot her by mistake.

Kodiak dens usually are located between 1,000 and 1,800 feet elevation, in open areas above or on the fringes of the brush line. Sometimes dens are located in small clearings, but often near alders. The animals seem to prefer dens located in steep terrain, with slopes between 40 and 60 degrees. Some experts claim that bruins prefer dens facing north, others say south. The truth is, on Kodiak at least, Brown Bears are likely to den on slopes facing any direction.

The big bears astound most experts by existing for five months without food or water. These animals have the ability to become so nearly lifeless during hibernation that they consume only minute amounts of stored energy each day. Hibernating bears exist in a lethargized stupor so intense that it could be compared to the comatose state. Yet, they remain alive. The bears lose considerable weight during hibernation while consuming six-inch layers of fat. They apparently continue breathing very slightly, and their bodies do give off heat. Because these body functions result in moisture vapors, frost forms on den walls, and steam sometimes can be seen rising from airholes above.

Before the snow melts in early spring, dens can be very hard to spot from the ground. Later, if the animals are the least bit active, dens can be located by glassing for disturbed patches of snow, or even patches of mud on top of any remaining snow. Sometimes after a bear has risen from its den, it will sleep for several days outside in the open. If this is the case, and the den is not otherwise evident, the bear can be mistaken for a large rock and overlooked. Even experienced guides do this on occasion.

Some bears, especially sows with cubs, remain close to their dens for weeks before moving to lower elevations. When bears do this, they usually lie on beds in the snow chewing on alders, and other trees and shrubs found nearby. The juices they suck from these plants apparently act as natural laxatives and help the animals get their digestive tracts functioning normally. Once bears leave their dens, however, they're usually gone for the season. Bears that den on one side of Kodiak may migrate to the opposite side during the summer months.

Bears seemingly have enough energy to run around the island every year, but I was fatigued when I trudged into the ADF&G cabin by the mouth of the Ayakulik. Fair weather enabled me to enjoy the day-long trek. My legs ached when I removed my hip boots that evening. However, my comfortable down mummy bag soon made me forget the unpleasant sensation, and I relaxed for a badly needed night's rest.

CHAPTER XI

Smoke curled from the Ayakulik cabin's chimney while I reeled in several plump Dolly Varden trout the next morning. The air was noisy with mosquitoes and seagulls. Magpies scolded loudly. An amazing variety of waterfowl flew overhead. There were Mergansers, Pintails and Mallards. A pair of Harlequin ducks also buzzed past me at low level on their way up the Ayakulik's course. Kodiak has a large waterfowl population, and many species are residents there year-round. As many as 40 species of ducks, geese, and swans have been recorded in the area. Some of these provide fine sport for local hunters.

There were other birds near the Ayakulik that morning. Two Bald Ealges gracefully soared overhead searching for food. Kodiak has an enormous population of these birds throughout the year. Eagle nests are very common on all parts of the island. Totally protected by federal law, they enjoy the same sort of supremacy in the air that they did on the east coast of our nation before the Pilgrims landed at Plymouth Rock. Life has been bumpy for the eagle ever since then, even on Kodiak. Before the federal law prohibiting eagle killing was passed, the big birds were killed for bounty in Alaska. Pinnell still recalls those days.

"In those days," he says, "we collected a bounty of two bits apiece for eagle claws from the government. Like everyone else, Morris and

I collected this bounty whenever we happened to get shots at the birds. One day we had a large collection of the claws ready for redemption when a friend, who had just come from town, advised us of the new law. He told us we'd better forget about the bounty and put distance between ourselves and those claws, or they would get us into the jackpot. Up until then, we knew nothing about the new law; we certainly didn't intend to break any law. So we got rid of the claws and haven't bothered eagles since. I doubt the bounty had any effect on the number of eagles, anyway. We've never noticed any difference — with or without it. But, I think the law protecting them is a good thing, especially down south where they've almost been exterminated.''

As an illustration of how many eagles inhabit Kodiak, P & T point out that "Eagle Creek," at the west end of Akalura Lake, was given its name after the two guides counted 74 eagles waiting there for a late run of Silver Salmon. Such sightings are not uncommon on Kodiak Island. The big birds thrive on Kodiak and no longer fear the presence of man. This was apparent when the two birds I watched finally settled on a nearby knoll and cast envious eyes on the trout I carried to the cabin.

Eagles weren't the only predatory creatures in the area. A bear's presence was evidenced by fresh tracks near the river. Seven-inch tracks clearly demonstrated its eight-foot size. The animal had walked within 100 feet of the cabin, apparently unafraid of my presence. Although the animals always concern outdoorsmen in bear country, nearby Kodiaks really aren't too dangerous so long as one respects their presence.

Some writers have zeroed in on the negative aspects of the big bear's personality. They have emphasized all of the bloody bear stories that they can locate in order to impress the public with a sense of terror. While I certainly encourage people who wander into bear country to be prepared, to carry adequate weapons, and to exhibit a healthy respect for the big beast, I believe that too much fear of bears can be unhealthy.

There certainly have been scores of deadly bear attacks on humans in Alaska since the turn of the century. But if one compares the number of those incidents with the hundreds of thousands, perhaps millions, of instances when the big bears have avoided contact with humans, it becomes obvious that the animals aren't lurking about looking for human chops. P & T probably have spent more time with

Kodiaks than any two humans on the face of the earth, and they've been in the direct path of more than their share of oncoming bruins, but they are rather quiet about charging bears. Listening to them recount their many experiences is the best way to discover the reason why.

"A lot of times bears have run toward me, but I can't say that they charged — they simply ran toward me," Talifson explains. "Just because a bear runs toward you doesn't mean that it is charging *at you*. If you fire and hit a bear, and it doesn't know where the shot came from or where you're at, but you happen to be between the bear and its most obvious route of escape, it probably will run straight toward you. But it won't be 'charging'; it will simply be trying to escape. However, if you don't knock the bear down before it reaches you, it may attack when it discovers you're there.

"I had one bear up at the east end of Akalura that did this. We were sitting on a high bank on the mountainside where the grass is real tall, and the bear walked right out beneath us just a few yards away before the hunter shot. When the hunter shot, the bear turned and ran right up the bank toward where we sat concealed in the grass. Well, the hunter's rifle jammed and there we sat — he couldn't make a second shot — and the bear came right up over the bank. It was less than five yards from us, so I was forced to shoot it from the hip. My shot knocked the bear over backwards, and it rolled to the bottom, giving my hunter a chance to recover and finish it off.

"There was another bear at Karluk Lake, however, that I had to shoot twice. I *know* that it charged. My hunter shot the bear right on the open beach and knocked it down; it got up and came right for us. I looked at the hunter and his gun was jammed. The bear was getting pretty close so I tried to just knock it down, because I didn't want to kill it for the hunter. Well, I knocked it down, but the bear got up again and here it came — right for us, popping its jaws as it came. The hunter still was fiddling with his gun, and by that time the bear was getting right on us. So I thought, 'well, I'd better do something this time,' and that time I knocked it down hard; but the bear still kept coming. Fortunately, the hunter got his rifle unjammed in time to finish off the bear just before I could shoot a third time. I think we stepped out 16 paces from where we stood to where the bear died.

"I had another close call," Talifson continues, "that was at least as close as that one. The hunter was down below me a ways; we were tracking a bear in the snow, and I was up a little higher on the mountain looking at tracks. The boar was with a sow and the rutting season was in full swing.

"We had seen the bears lying on a bench up on the mountain. So we climbed up there — it took us two hours because the mountain was so steep. When we got up to where we figured they should be, I thought I spotted them lying in an alder patch not far from the bench. But what I spotted wasn't the bears at all; it turned out to be boulders. Well, there weren't any bears there. But there was some green growth coming up a little further, so we went over and picked up the bears' tracks in the green stuff.

"We then followed those tracks around the mountain, but we separated about a hundred yards apart up and down the hill. The hunter was walking in the middle between me and my packer. So we went around the hill, and there was a little dip up next to the top. I started to pass up the dip, but decided to check it out.

"Just as I got up to the little dip to look, well there they were. The boar heard me coming and thought I was another boar about to challenge him for his sow. So here he came down the hill running right for me. I turned around and hollered at the hunter. When I did that, my upper false teeth flew out of my mouth. Fortunately, the hunter happened to turn around as I swooped up my teeth, threw them back into my mouth, and waved in a single motion for him to come up. Then I chambered a shell!

"Well, here this darned bear was coming after me, and I would look at the bear, then at the hunter, then at the bear, and I wasn't sure which one would get to me first! As luck would have it, my hunter got up where I was just as the bear was coming over the edge to come down on me. When the bear looked and saw two of us standing there, it stopped and stood up. That's when the hunter shot and knocked it over. That one fell pretty close to me too. But the hunter had said he wanted to shoot his own bear and didn't want me to even shoot at it. Otherwise, I might not have waited so long before I would have shot the bear myself.

"Well, when we started to skin the boar out, the sow came down to where we were and wouldn't leave. She sat about 50 or 60 feet from us, watching and growling. So finally I turned and told her

I'd 'had enough of that.' Then I ran over toward her and chased her out of there. She took off.

"Earlier," Talifson says, "after we'd gotten another bear, we had a very interesting and funny encounter with a bear. We had skinned the other hunter's trophy, and the packer and hunter went down to a creek to wash the blood from their hands and arms. Pretty soon, I heard brush popping and one of them hollered, 'Bear! Bear!' They came running back to us because they had no rifles. They had gotten down there and were washing their hands when they looked up and there came a bear right across the creek from them. My packer was scared of bears anyway, so they both came running.

"Then we all went over there, and I looked at the bear. It had a big rubbed spot on its back. So I told my other hunter that it wasn't a bear he would want. But he'd been wanting to get a good close-up picture of a bear, and I told him to get his camera ready. We got behind a big cottonwood tree right on the creek bank. We were standing there, and I said, 'I think he's gonna come right across right where we are. Just wait a minute.'

"Pretty soon here it came — the bear crossed the creek and got up on the bank right beside us. So I whispered to the hunter, 'Be ready. I'll get the bear to stand up and you just swing around the tree and snap your picture.' Then I snapped a branch and the bear stood up. But when the hunter stuck his head around the tree and saw the bear so darned close, he got scared, dropped his camera, grabbed his rifle, and lost his picture! Funniest thing was, that the poor bear was just as shocked to see the hunter as the hunter was to see it so close. The bear took off pretty fast, too!

"Years ago," Talifson continues, "I had one close call that I'll never forget. We'd gotten one bear, and I sent the hide back to camp with the packers after we found tracks of a very large bear. This animal apparently had been spooked out of the grass where it was hidden when we shot the first bear. The big tracks went up into the pass between Red Lake and the (Ayakulik) flats. The packers wanted to follow the lowland route, so I and the hunters went up the pass after the big bear.

"The bear went into one little willow patch, so we went around to the other side where I saw that it had come out. Then we went up into the pass a little further, and the bear had passed through a second willow patch. Finally, the bear's tracks entered a third *big*

155

willow patch, and we started to go around it. Part-way around, there was a narrow alleyway, right through the middle of the patch. So we went down there to see if the bear had passed from one section of the patch to the other. It had, and I was just turning around to get us out of there when my hunter said, 'I can smell the bear!''

"So, I got down on my hands and knees and looked up through the hole in the brush where the bear had gone. There it was standing there looking at us — not 12 feet away! I whispered to my hunter to load his gun, and that I'd get the bear to stand up.

"So then I got the bear to stand up. It was just standing there above the brush looking down at us. But my hunter didn't shoot. When I looked around, he was fiddling with his rifle — his scope cover was tangled up. Then he tried to load his rifle and had trouble doing that, too. Finally I said, 'You're gonna have to hurry because the bear won't stand there all day!' So he fired and hit the bear low in the chest, missing its backbone. The bear came right down off its hind feet facing us, and I thought, 'It's coming our way!' I was ready, so I just fired into the brush, hoping to slow it down anyway. Fortunately, the bear turned when it hit the ground and ran the other way.

That same year, I had been trying to see just how close I could get hunters up on bears. This big bear was just 12 feet. After that, I figured I'd gotten *close enough*. If it had broken out on us, we wouldn't have had a chance in the world. We'd have had quite an awful time stopping the bear before it got one of us. The second hunter with us had his movie camera ready, but in the excitement he threw down his camera and grabbed his rifle. Things almost got out of hand on us.''

Bill Pinnell also has had his share of close encounters with Kodiaks. The closest call that he enjoys talking about involved a bear that weighed at least 1,407 pounds.

"The reason we know how much it weighed," he explains, "is that the Fish and Wildlife people showed up and offered to pack the hide out if we'd let them cut up the bear and weigh it.

"The way we happened onto the bear was that Morris had taken one hunter around some brush one way, and I and a packer had taken the other hunter around the other way. Morris and his hunter spooked the bear. It ran around the brush, spotted us, and charged. My packer didn't have a rifle, and the hunter had a semi-automatic 30-06. This bear was coming and I was hollering, 'Shoot! Shoot! Shoot!' But the hunter just stood there shaking. Finally, I couldn't wait any longer. My packer was poking me in the back and muttering words that I shouldn't repeat. So I shot and hit the bear in the shoulder. That slowed the bear down and turned it sideways. I shot it a second time, and this time it went down pretty hard. About that time, the hunter came to life with his 30-06, and you would have thought it was a Gatling gun.

"After he killed the bear, the hunter started prancing around saying, "My goodness, three minutes ago I didn't think I was gonna get a bear, and just think, it's happened to me, it's happened to me — didn't think I would get a bear and it's happened to me, it's happened to me.'

"My packer and I measured the distance from where we had been standing to the place it had first been hit — it measured just 27 feet. My packer told me, 'I thought you'd never pull that trigger!' You get 27 feet from a bear that's coming on high, and it's *really* something, let me tell you!

"Another time," Pinnell continues, "I and Gene Maye were coming back from Fraser Lake when we ran into a bear in a little opening up by Akalura. We were wearing old yellow rain slickers like they used to sell at canneries. Boy! When that bear saw us, it came tearing out of the brush on high, and I don't mean maybe. It came out and stopped a little ways away, and started stomping its feet, huffing, puffing and popping its jaws. Gene was left-handed and a poor shot. I had a shotgun and he had a 30-06. I figured the bear was bluffing, but I wasn't sure.

"Gene said, 'If it comes another step, I'm gonna let him have it!'

"'Don't you dare,' I told him.

"'If it comes any closer, I'm gonna let him have it,' Gene repeated.

"'Don't you dare shoot it!' I said. This continued several minutes.

"Well what I did — I had some matches and I lit three fires. The grass was wet and wouldn't burn very good. It would burn a little patch, you know. But the bear just stood there — it huffed and puffed and snorted, and watched the grass burn. Finally, the bear went back in the brush, but several seconds later it came out again.

"Well, the bear huffed, puffed, and blowed, but it couldn't scare

157

us out, and it went back in the brush again. Then a few minutes later it came out on a little ridge about 200 yards away and just stood there watching us. Now just how mad the bear was, or whether it had a sore foot, sore tongue or a toothache, I'll never know. But it sure had us worried for awhile."

"Another time," says Pinnell, "Morris and I were picking berries up on the hill behind Eagle Creak — over near Grass Valley. We had a black dog that we called 'Mike.' Well, Mike was over the hill, and he started barking to beat the band. There was a fox den over there, and we figured he was after the foxes. Mike kept on barking, and finally I thought, 'Well, I'll go over there and run Mike away from the fox den.' So, I went over the ridge and about that time — about 200 yards from me — here came old Mike running on high about as fast as he could. And about 200 yards behind Mike was a bear!

"So boy, I took out for Morris. Morris had the old 30-30. I was just yards from Morris when he saw me coming.

"'Mike's got a bear!' I hollered.

"Then Morris held out his pail of berries to me and shouted, 'Take the gun! Take the gun!'

"Morris wasn't the least bit scared, see. I already had a pail of berries of my own, and that was enough for me! So we cut out and headed up the mountain a ways.

"Old Mike caught up with us when the bear came over the ridge about 75 yards away. We weren't sure what the bear would do. It stopped when it saw us, and huffed and puffed and snorted at us. Finally I hollered at the bear, and it stopped making noise. But its old bristles were raised up on the back of its legs when it walked away. Mike sure got under that bear's skin, and the bear almost got ours in return!

"But," says Pinnell, "I can't say that I ever saw a truly *mean* bear. Bears get upset just like people do, and that's when they get into trouble with people. As a rule they don't harm anything if they're left alone.

"When I was trapping way out in the flats, there was a big bear that used to lie down in the trail outside my tent while I was away. It never molested my camp. The bear probably knew, see, when we showed up, that it shouldn't hang around like that, and it would go somewhere else. But after we'd leave, it would always come back and lie down in the same place. It would just lay out in front of our camp like a big dog and keep an eye on things. I guess you could say that we had an *understanding*.

"The biggest problem sometimes is the human's fear of bears. Some people have an uncontrollable fear of bears," says Pinnell. "I had one hunter I remember who missed his bear for that reason. The bear was up on the hill, and I thought we could get the hunter to sit down and shoot. But when the hunter sat down he couldn't see the bear, and by that time he was *shaking* all over — just shaking all over.

"So I said, 'Shoot!'

"But the hunter didn't shoot; and he said, 'Do you want me to shoo—shoo—,shoo—oot?'

"'Yes shoot'

"Then, the hunter went through that again. He said, 'Do you want me to shoo—, shoo—, shoo—oot?'

"'Shoot!'

"That time my packer started laughing, so I poked him in the side and told him to 'shut up.'

"'Do you want me to shoo—, shoo—, shoo—oot?' he said again. 'Yes, for cripe' sake, shoot!' I said.

"Well he finally shot; but he missed because the barrel of his rifle was doing cartwheels.

"We had a doctor with us, and I said, 'Doc, don't you dare go back to camp and tell this on him.' 'Oh, I wouldn't do that!' he told me. 'He's one of the best friends I've got!'

"That night when we got into camp, the hunter admitted to the others what had happened.

"'Well,' he said, 'I could have had a nice bear today, but I got shakitis and lost it.'"

Morris Talifson had an experience with a shaky hunter that wasn't funny when it occurred. In fact, it was frightening.

"We were out hunting when my packer spotted a bear heading up toward Eagle Creek," Talifson explains. "It was a nine-foot bear, so we headed up the creek for it. The animal had lain down in the brush by the time we got across a ridge that separated us from it. So I climbed a little knob to look for the bear. But while I was climing, it must have seen me, because it got up and headed for the hill on the back side of Eagle Creek. Well, I ran back down the knob, and we watched the bear move up into a higher alder patch where it bedded again. This time I took the hunter and we began to stalk.

"We hadn't gone far when we ran into a long stretch of open grass. While we were crossing the grass, the bear spotted us and took off running.

"So I told the hunter, 'You better take it!'

"He shot, but he didn't kill the bear, and it wobbled down into some alders. So I told the hunter to follow me over to the bear and finish it off. I got down there about 30 yards from the bear, and there it was — it stood up and was growling at me. But when I told the hunter to shoot, he didn't, and I turned around only to discover that he wasn't there! He was standing back up on the hill about 200 yards away — watching me.

"So I hollered at the hunter and told him to come down and kill the bear. He didn't want to come down, but finally I got him down there. This time he shot again, but didn't do any good, and the bear turned and went deeper into the alders.

"Well, I started on after the bear again — I thought the hunter would follow me this time. But when I got to the bear and told the hunter to shoot, nothing happened. He'd stayed behind again. The bear was starting to get really angry by now. It was growling and jumping at me on its front feet the way bears do. So I hollered at the hunter again.

"'*Get down here!*' I yelled.

"The hunter finally came on down, but he was dragging. By this time the bear was growling even louder and popping its jaws as it stomped its feet. About the time the hunter got there and I told him to shoot, the bear grabbed a five-inch-thick alder limb with its mouth, split it in two, and tore about half of it off with a single jerk of its head!

"I looked at the hunter when the bear did that, and he was white as a sheet! The hunter was completely *unnerved*. He was weaving back and forth, and was so unsteady that when I told him to shoot

160

again he couldn't even hit the bear just yards away. Then the animal retreated even further into the alders.

"So I told the hunter, 'This time you *stay with me!*'

"We followed the bear, and it had really gone into a jungle. We were forced to crawl on our hands and knees a few times, but I finally found the bear in a little open spot. When the bear saw us coming, it stood up as if it knew what to expect. My hunter shot again, but he couldn't hit the bear, which was badly hurt. So I finally broke its neck with my .375.

"There are a few times when wounded bears really express themselves in ways that are difficult to describe," Talifson continues. "Another one of my hunters shot a bear between Akalura and Fraser lakes. He broke the bear's back, and it rolled down the hill into a gully. We went over there to finish it off, and boy, oh boy — if there ever was such a thing as hate — that bear *just glared* at me! I couldn't stand to look at the bear. I told my hunter, 'Break its neck!' Then I turned around and looked the other way until the bear was dead. That bear *just glared* at me! No other bear I remember ever gave me that kind of look. It was an old boar — well over ten feet in size."

People are attacked by bears almost every year in Alaska, but most authorities will admit that almost all of the incidents to date could have been avoided if the persons involved had recognized that they were breaking some Brown Bear rule or code of etiquette. Like humans, bears have their own expectations regarding acceptable behavior. While humans probably never will fully comprehend all of the reasons why individual bears attack, a few guidelines that can help one to avoid most problems are in order.

"In the first place," Talifson warns, "one should always keep a clean camp. Garbage, expecially meat scraps, is the biggest cause of bear problems. Burn what you can burn, and then sink the ashes and what won't burn in a lake or bay where it won't smell. Bears can smell food that is buried in the ground."

Along the same line, don't store meat inside cabins or tents. Always keep it outdoors. Deer or other game meat always should be hung *away* from your living shelter. Another tent can be used for that purpose — but don't live in it with the meat. Bears become violently possessive any time they claim food. It may be your meat, but the bear that claims it will attack you if it feels challenged for possession.

Also, always carry a flashlight after dark so bears will see you and clear out if they can't otherwise detect your presence by smell or sound. They almost always clear out if they know you're nearby.

Another thing to remember is to avoid brushy areas where your view of the country is restricted. These areas are dangerous because of the high risk of surprising bears at close range. You can avoid a lot of brush by picking trails high on mountainsides.

If you're forced to walk through brush, and you aren't *hunting* for bears, you should whistle, sing or make some kind of noise so that bears will hear you and clear out. Some folks carry cowbells and that sort of thing.

"If a bear gets after you and you can't climb a tree," Talifson says, "don't try to run away from it. You can't outrun a bear. Simply face the bear. Yell at it. Throw it your coat and any other belongings you have with you — once piece at a time. This may appease the animal long enough for you to back away very cautiously. Be careful not to stumble."

"Most of the time a bear will bluff," Pinnell adds. "When a bear is bluffing it usually will stomp its feet and snort at you. The sound of a snorting bear is like 'sheuu, sheuu.' It may sound serious, but a serious snort is different than a bluffing snort. The serious snort has a lot more behind it — a lower-pitched sound, but you won't be able to tell the difference unless you've first heard a bear bluffing."

CHAPTER XII*

I stayed at the Ayakulik cabin several days before heading back to the Olga Bay cannery. During that time I gave much thought to the various kinds of modern camp outfits that people bring with them to Brown Bear country.

In the old days, the sage advice was to carry nothing but a rifle, hatchet, belt knife, blanket roll, fishing line with hooks, and a few staples. Some guides, such as the immortal Andy Simons, carried such outfits. But many things have changed since the days when iron men roamed at will throughout the far north. We have many options today that those hardy souls never dreamed of. Oldtimers like P & T attest that many of these options are worthwhile, too, even though the two sometimes laugh at items carried by greenhorns. Personally, I believe hunters should outfit for comfort, with due regard to practicality. Many gadgets are useful but unnecessary. Others are too heavy or bulky. One must distinguish between "roughing it" and "ruining it" when planning an enjoyable trip afield, and try not to do both at the same time.

There probably aren't any better outfitters than P & T, yet those two aren't known for fancy camps. P & T are known for providing *comfortable* camps and *successful* hunts. The pair developed many

This chapter contains detailed information about hunting camp outfitting. If not interested, it can be skipped.

of their outfitting skills during the Great Depression when they were forced to make do with whatever was handy. Consequently, they learned how to make simple outfits more comfortable than the inexperienced might imagine. And because of their expertise, and my experience working for them, I have adopted many P & T outfitting habits as the basis for my own notions on the subject. The following is a summary of the ideas I've gathered for outfitting hunting camps.

The Grub List

Dehydrated Food. Unless a hunter plans to backpack more than 10 miles from the end of mechanized transportation, I see little value in packing dehydrated food. This certainly is a personal preference, because there are advantages to having a light pack. However, I do not agree with dehydrated food because the stuff simply doesn't turn my taste buds. If dehydrated food is desired, one probably can determine the amount he needs by relying upon the information printed on the packages.

For shorter distances afield, I prefer conventional food stocks even though more weight is involved. Conventional meals are tastier and more filling. Approximately 45-50 pounds of food will last a hard-working man two weeks. Unless he is packing farther than 10 miles, a man should be capable of packing that much weight. If he can't, he should consider other options.

Camp Meat.   Camp meat often is not a problem in Alaska, at least where deer and caribou are found. But many areas have few meat animals; and if one is trophy hunting for bear, he shouldn't be shooting other species at the outset, because he'll scare the more desirable bruins out of the country by doing so.

In any event, a hunting camp shouldn't be entirely dependent upon wild game. Hard-working men require at least a pound of steak or hamburger, per man, per day. But beef may not be practical while packing cross-country, and trout might be the mainstay.

Slab bacon is one item that ought to be in every camp. Four pounds per man per week is plenty. Stay away from canned and pre-sliced bacon if possible. These are expensive, and sometimes don't keep too well. Bacon grease should be saved in some sort of container. It is used for frying hotcakes, etc. Bacon rind is useful in beans and other foods, too.

Some hunters complain that slicing slab bacon is troublesome. Slab bacon is easiest to slice when cold, or slightly frozen. I slice slab bacon before separating it from the rind. I cut the slices down to the rind, without slicing through the rind. Then, when all of my slices are cut, I free them from the rind by running my knife blade flat against the rind under the slices.

Some blades are worthless for slicing bacon. But the *Kershaw* stainless steel "camp kit" contains a blade that is excellent for the purpose. This knife set is also very compact. There may be other blades on the market that are good, too. One that comes to mind is the "crooked knife" that Herter's, Inc. used to sell. Nowadays the only source for these may be through the Green River Works. That company sells crooked knife kits under the *Russel* label.

P & T are famous for the *Spam* sandwiches that they serve with soup. Spam packs well in the field and is a welcome emergency ration when one is forced to stay out all night. I usually include several cans of Spam in my own outfit.

Vegetables. The only fresh vegetables that I bother with are onions and potatoes. Two pounds of onions will suffice on most hunting trips. Five pounds of fresh potatoes per man per week usually is sufficient. Potatoes can be boiled, baked, or sliced and fried in bacon grease with diced onion.

Dehydrated vegetables are useful for soups and stews, but canned vegetables are important. There should be an equal number of peas, green beans, and corn. Others to consider are stewed tomatoes, asparagus, beets, butter beans, carrots, etc. As a rule, one should pack three-quarters of a can per man per day.

Dried Beans, Cereals, Rice, Etc. Pinto beans are my favorite. I also enjoy navy and lima beans. I do not care for, nor do I pack, kidney beans because of their tough skins. However, as a rule, the larger the bean is, the faster it cooks. Beans can be soaked all day while you hunt, and cooked late at night after dinner. Then they are ready for meals the next day. Beans seem to get better every time they're warmed over. I usually add lots of bacon to my beans. The rind is soft and tasty by the time the beans are cooked. Sliced onion is also a good bean additive.

Two good cereals are cracked wheat and Cream of Wheat. These are light and filling. I enjoy either of these late at night before turning in; but they're excellent breakfast items, too. Covered with butter, sugar, and milk, these cereals pack a lot of punch for any hungry bear hunter.

Whether measuring beans, rice, macaroni, or whatever, P & T

taught me that one good fistful per man per meal is plenty. One pound of dried beans per man per week is the minimum I carry; beans are so light that any error on the side of excess is beneficial, and can be a lifesaver in an emergency. A pound of rice and eight ounces of macaroni per man per week should also be packed.

Flour, Etc. Ordinarily I carry no more than five pounds of regular white flour. I use it for coating fish, ptarmigan, etc. before frying. I also pack at least five pounds of prepared pancake mix per man per week, and use it for everything from pancakes to biscuits and cornbread. One pound of cornmeal per man per week is necessary for the latter purpose. For cornbread, I mix no more than 40 percent cornmeal with prepared pancake mix. I add *plenty* of sugar, and double the number of eggs called for by most recipes.

Eggs, Bread, Etc. Real eggs and store-bought white bread always are best. One large loaf per man per week is enough bread in most cases, but two loaves will be necessary if French toast is desired.

Three dozen eggs per man per week are sufficient. I have never tried powdered egg mixes. These aren't as useful as fresh eggs and must be mixed with vegetable oil, etc., for proper blending.

Milk Products and Beverages. Powdered milk is handy and pretty good for general drinking. It is a good substitute for canned milk in a number of recipes, too.

At least a pound of cheese per man should be packed. Cheese is necessary for macaroni dishes and sandwiches. One pound of real butter per man per two weeks is also necessary.

About three pounds of coffee and a half pound of tea will satisfy most bear camps. If there are several heavy coffee drinkers in camp, carry an extra can. One usually can bring home, or cache in the field, any supplies that are left over. However, left-over tea usually is bitter after a few months of storage.

Miscellaneous Items. Canned fruit: one 29-ounce can per two men per day is necessary. I like a variety of peaches, apricots, pears or prunes.

A large bottle of catsup and a medium-size tin of shortening, will meet most bear camp needs. I pack plenty of shortening because it is so necessary for frying fish and fowl. I seldom fry steak in shortening; I prefer to fry steak on top of a liberal application of table salt.

A large jar of peanut butter, and several two- or three-pound cans of the finest jam obtainable, should always be packed. Don't be cheap on jam. Quality counts here, as has been learned by every major field army in the world.

A five-pound bag of sugar is convenient for a two-man camp. If syrup will be made in camp, ten pounds may be necessary. A pound or two of raisins is handy for snacks as well as recipes. Also, two pounds of candy bars per man per week preferred.

If all of the items mentioned above are taken, you'll wind up with a pretty hefty load of over 60 pounds. Actually, 45 pounds of food will be ample for one hard working man on a two-week hunt. However, it is easy to get weathered in in Alaska, so one should plan for that to happen. An oldtimer offered the best advice when he said, "You should figure all the food you think you will need, and then *double* it." Anyone who has ever been forced to forage for food while weathered in will appreciate that rule. A friend of mine went gold prospecting in February with a two-week supply of food. He wound up stranded a total of four weeks, and had to shoot deer out of season in order to eat. He learned a valuable lesson.

The following is a sample list of provisions for one person on a one-week stint where weight is not a problem:

Quantity		Item
7	lbs.	beef
3	lbs.	slab bacon
3	cans	soup
2	oz.	dehydrated soup
1	lb.	butter
1	lb.	cheese
6	oz.	shortening
12	oz.	powdered milk
5	lbs.	pancake mix (self-rising)
1	lb.	cornmeal
4	oz.	macaroni
6	oz.	rice
1	lb.	dried beans
1	lb.	wheat cereal (cream or cracked)
1	lb.	dried potato slices (equal to 5 lbs. fresh)
1	lb.	onions
5	cans	vegetables

2	cans (16-oz.)	fruit
8	oz.	raisins
1	lb.	peanut butter
3	lb.	sugar
2	lb.	candy
2	lb.	jam
8	oz.	coffee
1	oz.	tea
1	oz.	salt (more if needed for hides)
1	oz.	pepper

Camp Cookery

The cooking gear that one should take along depends upon the nature of the trip. If backpacking, a one-burner stove and light aluminum pan set is best. However, average hunters have no reason *not* to carry better equipment.

The ordinary camp should be equipped with at least one two-burner gas cook stove. I have no use for the propane models. If living in a wall tent or cabin, some sort of small, light-weight woodstove (one that weighs under 35 pounds) is also preferable. A wall tent can be fitted with a stovepipe collar, and most cabins are built to accomodate stovepipes. Don't trust oil stoves that are installed in some recreation cabins. Some of them don't work. If one is not a woodstove fan, some kind of catalytic heater may be useful, but more fuel will be needed. In my opinion, any camp without a woodstove is less than the best.

P & T use a sheepherder-type woodstove. It is about three feet long, eighteen inches wide, and one foot deep. It is made of ordinary sheetmetal, and uses a six-inch stovepipe. Its surface buckles and bends after a little use, but it will last for three or four seasons. P & T camps are warm, and meals cooked on those stoves almost never fail. Such a stove should be set on top of a couple of empty gas cans for stability (make sure the cans don't contain any gas fumes!). If the camp is equipped with a woodstove, ten gallons white gas and five gallons of stove oil will last ten days to two weeks. The stove oil is used to start the wood stove burning each morning, and to start green wood burning. The white gas, of course, is for appliances.

If weight permits, a ten-inch cast-iron skillet, and a cast-iron, or heavy aluminum, griddle for pancakes will significantly improve the camp menu. Most aluminum "camp" griddles are too light to ensure uniform distribution of heat. Pancakes on one end may burn while those at the other are still raw. Light-weight griddles warp badly, too.

A dutch oven would be a real luxury. If you'd like to cook your beans while you're out hunting, and there's no one in camp to feed the stove, a dutch oven could be the ticket. I've never carried one on any of my own hunts, but I recognize their value.

A full set of pots is very desirable. A two- or three-quart pot and several smaller ones will suffice. A small pan to be used as a water dipper should never be left behind. Also, a ten-cup aluminum coffee pot and a large tea kettle are necessary. Three five-gallon pails, two for water and one for garbage, are sufficient for a three or four man camp.

Don't include paper, plastic or tin plates unless backpacking. Tin cups should be avoided at all costs; these are good only for burning lips. Any diningware suitable for regular home use probably is fit for a hunting camp. The camp outfit should contain an egg turner, at least a couple of large tablespoons, and any other kitchen utensils that may be handy. If you hunt in the same area each year, you can cache a complete cookery outfit in the field for annual use. A little common sense when choosing a site for the cache will prevent most thefts during the off-seasons.

Shelter

Cabins. Cabins are not always available to hunters — even in Alaska. The U.S. Fish and Wildlife Service maintains some cabins on its refuges. But these often are assigned to parties on a drawing permit basis, and the drawings are not correlated with similar drawings for state hunting permits. The inevitable result is that persons drawing a permit for one, may not draw a permit for the other. Therefore, don't count on a Fish and Wildlife cabin even though there may be one in your area.

The Forest Service also maintains cabins in prime locations. These may offer the opportunity an individual needs and should be considered. Other cabins do exist, but should not be used without permission, except in an emergency.

Tents. Bill Pinnell says, "It takes a real man to hunt from a tent on Kodiak in November." Pinnell speaks from first-hand knowledge because he certainly has spent many of his 45 Novembers on Kodiak Island doing just that. Although Kodiak winters may not demonstrate the low temperatures that other parts of Alaska are famous for, its winters are just as harsh. Gale-force winds in excess of 100 knots are common. These may also exist in conjunction with sub-zero temperatures. *If* your tent is not blown away, you'd better have a good stove to keep the chill off.

There are many "expedition" tents on the market that manufacturers claim will withstand strong wind. Some of these may be good. P & T always have relied on old-fashioned 9 x 12 wall tents with sod cloths. Properly erected, wall tents are comfortable and stable. Wall tents intended for hunting camp use should be fitted with separate tarpaulin floors and stovepipe collars. The stovepipe collar always should be located near the door so that wood won't need to be hauled all the way to the rear. A 9 x 12 wall tent made of ten-ounce canvas weighs about 35 pounds. Poles of some kind usually are available on site or nearby.

Although tent flies sometimes catch wind, they do assure dryness and warmth. During November, you should expect cold, damp weather at best, and blizzards at worst. So, unless weight is a big factor, a fly should be seriously considered.

Ideally, two full-sized wall tents should be used. That way, all storage and cooking can be assigned to one tent, and hunters can sleep in the other. As a practical matter, however, most ordinary hunters will be doing well to have a single wall tent augmented with a light-weight, cheap two-man tent for storage, etc.

Miscellaneous Camp Gear. Gasoline lanterns are the handiest inventions since paper clips. Small models can be obtained for backpacking. I do not like propane models; I detest the inevitable accumulation of empty fuel containers.

Be certain to bring an extra generator and several mantles for the gas lantern. Pack a few candles, at least one good flashlight per man, with extra bulbs, and four sets of flashlight batteries per man.

Stout wooden boxes are worth their weight in gold. They become camp furniture the moment they're emptied. The wooden "blazo" boxes used a decade ago were perfect, but oil companies discontinued using square gas cans, as well as the boxes they came in. If you don't have any of these boxes stored from "the good old days," you can make them out of lumber. Rope handles in both ends and a hinged lid should be added.

Clothing

Undergarments. Individuals vary a great deal regarding body warmth, etc. Along Alaska's coast, through mid-October, medium-weight cotton union suits are suitable. Hunters are advised to refrain from wearing underwear that is too heavy. Outer layers can be removed more easily than undergarments. One word to the wise: always buy cotton union suits at least *six* sizes too large in order to avoid "cutting" under the armpits after washing. Cotton union suits shrink a lot when washed.

I avoid two-piece insulated undergarments. They usually are too hot, and they create an uncomfortable "bundle" about my waist. After experiencing union suits, I've never been tempted to wear anything else. They're simply comfortable.

Pants. Although most jeans are appropriate, beware of tight-fitting patterns. I prefer loose-fitting khaki pants except during colder weather when I turn to wool. On Kodiak, if a union suit and one pair of khaki pants won't keep my legs warm, I simply pull up my hip boots and belt them to my waist. This adds a wind-proof layer of insulation.

I've always been amazed at how some individuals wind up becoming red hot because they wear too many heavy clothes. Some of P & T's clients have shed a lot of expensive garments less than 15 minutes from camp.

Shirts. On Kodiak, and elsewhere in Brown Bear country, a hunter is well advised to wear a heavy cotton or polyester-blend flannel shirt under a heavy wool jac shirt of some sort. The jac shirt can be quickly removed if the hunter becomes too warm, and quickly replaced if he gets too cold. I wear a jac shirt that has a long, tapered tail. This helps to keep my upper thighs warm. I do not wear wool jac shirts with linings because these are entirely too warm when hiking. I seldom wear my jac shirt when packing heavy loads. Sometimes I even remove my flannel shirt.

171

Coats. A fine expedition-grade down coat really is pleasant to have when sitting still or glassing. Warm down garments should always be shed when forced to move fast. If not removed, the wearer quickly overheats.

Vests. Down vests are valuable at all times.

Headgear. Stocking caps are warm, but many men prefer caps with bills. Always try to carry a raincoat with a hood. However, a seaman's rain hat can be used, and may permit a greater field of view over the shoulder.

Raingear. Always carry a pair of hip boots when hunting in Alaska. Coastal Alaska is simply too wet for leather boots. Even when sheep hunting, hip boots sometimes are a must. Avoid ankle-fitting hip boots if possible. P & T have learned that ankle-fitting hipboots cause blisters. They are also hard to remove in an emergency. A tire-patch kit probably will be needed. An old cut-off pair of hip boots makes a fine pair of camp shoes.

I don't care for rain pants. They're noisy and sometimes downright hot.

I've found that the lightest raincoats are best. I've gotten excellent mileage out of raincoats that cost less than five dollars. Avoid bright colors.

Socks. Always wear thick socks with hipboots. The best are those with at least 85 percent nylon content. 100 percent wool socks wear out too fast to be worthwhile except during extremely cold weather. I've increased the life of many wool socks by wearing thin nylon socks over them. An extra pair of heavy socks should be toted in the packsack, in case one gets cold or wet. Sometimes a fresh pair of socks at mid-day will add miles to one's endurance, too.

Belts and Suspenders. Belts are tiring because of the way they hang on the waist. A good pair of suspenders will help prevent fatigue in that respect. Greenhorns and those with macho complexes (as well as those who have never thought about it) clutter their waists with gadgets and bulky items. Anyone with very many miles on his boots usually will throw these things inside his packsack where they're out of the way.

Other Gear

Rifles. There are innumerable makes, models and calibers on the market, many of which are well suited for Brown Bear hunting. I prefer the .375 H & H magnum; it will belt you if you're out of shape and unaccustomed to the load, but it's as reliable as any cartridge on the market. The .375 H & H has a loud report which can cause flinching. Frequent practice is a must.

The 30-06 is the smallest rifle anyone ought to rely upon for big bear hunting. Some years ago, many hunters touted the 7 mm. magnum as the cure-all cartridge. But as Bill Pinnell says, "you've got to riddle the bear to kill it with a 7 mm. magnum." This is true, at least with large Brown Bears.

Spotting Scopes and Binoculers. A good spotting scope is a *must*. In any big game hunting, one's ability to scrutinize unidentifiable objects is critical. A 40-power scope is best for Brown Bear hunting, although I use a 20-power. Sixty-power scopes are too powerful for Kodiak terrain but are useful for sheep hunting elsewhere.

One doesn't need an expensive pair of binoculars. My own cost under 100 dollars. *Never* try to rely upon a rifle scope as a substitute for binoculars. A hunter is *greatly* handicapped without binoculars.

Pack Frames. Again, there are a number of good frames on the market. The secret is to find one that allows you to pack at least 100 pounds bulk.

Knives. Most guides carry large folding knives for skinning and fleshing. P & T carry such knives, and also pack the big "crooked" knives discussed earlier. These are best for fleshing bear hides. I also carry a smaller penknife with blades less than two inches long. This knife is best for "turning" ears, eyes and lips.

Miscellaneous Items. As stated earlier, one should never leave home without a flashlight. And it is wise to insert a piece of cardboard in front of the battery post to prevent accidental loss of charge while the light is in your pack. Always carry extra batteries in your pack, too. Three or four sets of batteries should be stocked.

Matches, toilet paper, etc. should always be carried inside waterproof containers when out in the field. Extra socks and gloves should also be carried.

Some other things that shouldn't be left at home are dishpans, dish towels, face cloths, body towels and soap. Leave your razor at home if this will enhance your self-image, but always take along a toothbrush. Even in the field, some hunters can be offended by foul breath.

CHAPTER XIII

Three-foot waves splashed salty brine at my feet as I trudged along the outside beach on my way to the head of Olga bay. I finally was returning to less remote country after a trek through the heart of Kodiak's bear country. My stay at the Ayakulik cabin had been pleasant. The soon-to-arrive weir attendants certainly would enjoy their summer at that cabin.

The boys who man the fish weirs along Alaska's coastline enjoy a choice slice of life. Although family men seldom are found in these jobs, younger men can enjoy the thrill of being isolated in the bush amid wild creatures, and still have all the comforts of civilization.

Like other ADF&G cabins on Kodiak, the one at the mouth of the Ayakulik is equipped with "soft" bunks and a propane cooking range. During summer months, a gas generator provides the occupants with electricity for radio and lights. Some other cabins even enjoy indoor showers. Weekly "grocery" flights provide the weir attendants with fresh produce and milk. A well equipped shop also permits the men to maintain equiment.

Once the weir is set up in the spring, the workers spend only a few hours each day working; most of their actual work time is spent monitoring water and weather conditions, and watching for salmon. Even when the salmon begin running, the fish are conveniently held behind the weir. When a large number are pressed behind the fence attempting to pass, the workers open a gate and count the fish as they pass.

During their spare time, weir attendants are allowed to hunt, fish, mine for gold, comb the beach, or participate in just about any enjoyable hobby they care to engage in. The men also enjoy free room and board, and are able to save small fortunes in just a few months' time. Needless to say, competition is keen for these jobs.

Weir attendants enjoyed less leisure in former years. P & T worked as weir attendants at the mouth of the Ayakulik during their early years on the island; and the U.S. Fish and Wildlife Service, which was in charge of Alaska's fisheries at that time, had no trouble filling their days with work. In fact, the Fish and Wildlife Service instructed the two to "eliminate" predatory Dolly Varden trout during their "spare" time.

"Dollies eat salmon eggs before they even hit the stream bed, and they also eat lots of the fry," Pinnell explains. "In those days there was a bounty on Dollies. At first, it was five cents a tail, and later it was reduced to two-and-a half cents a tail; but we had to kill the Dollies on our salary — we got no bounty. Morris and I each got paid only 150 dollars a month and we boarded ourselves.

"We killed a thousand Dollies a day for 90 days one season. We knew how many we killed by emptying our trap into a boat. There were marks in the boat, and when the fish were piled up to the right mark, we had a thousand fish. Nowadays, they don't kill Dollies, and we don't have as many salmon either. You'd think that the state Fish and Game people would get smart. Maybe someday they will."

Not far from the Ayakulik River I spotted a perfectly sound miner's cabin that certainly was in desperate straits. The little cabin literally was "hanging on for dear life," while the moraine bluff beneath it was being slowly eroded by each high tide. The structure was hanging off the edge of the 75-foot bluff as if ready to fall onto the beach at any moment. I paused to mourn the apparent passing of this cabin. Its demise signalled the changing political and economic winds of our time.

Cabins are worth a king's ransom on Kodiak. Ever since the national refuge was established on the island, new cabin construction has been carefully restricted. Most of the guides, including P & T, already owned cabins. These were permitted to remain. Gill-net fisher-

Ten-Footer taken after a light snow. Photograph courtesy of P & T collection.

Salting a field-fleshed bear hide.

At least seven spring Kodiaks hanging in open air after curing on the hidehouse floor.

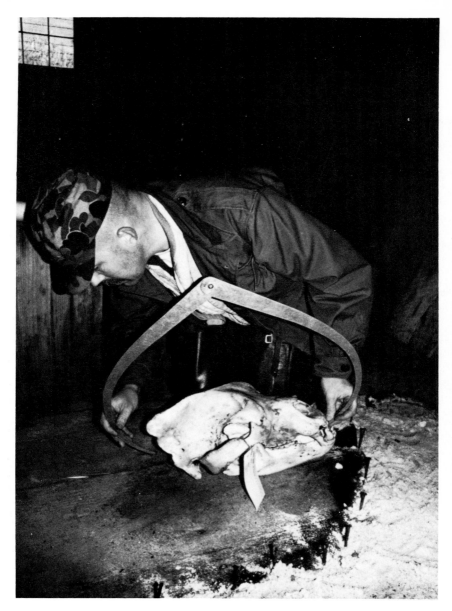

The refuge manager measures a trophy bear skull.

Here the P & T crew poses with three spring trophies. This photo was taken early in Pinnell's and Talifson's careers before the two began "square-skinning" hides. Note the bad rub on the center hide, above Bill Pinnell's head. Up to 50 percent of all Kodiak spring hides are rubbed, many quite badly. Photo courtesy of P & T collection.

In the old days, Kodiaks were hunted from September 1 until June 20. This bear was taken on an early September hunt. All of the animal's old fur had shed, except a small amount on the back of its neck. The rest of this hide was covered with short, new fur, which would have been fully grown out within two more months

The author, at age 18, with a few of the pelts taken on his trapline.

Bill Pinnell shakes hands with Tramp, Morris Talifson's dog. Note the Otter and Fox pelts in background.

Beautiful Olga Bay.

The four big retorts shown in this picture were "state of the art" when the Olga Bay cannery was built in 1890.

Morris Talifson enjoys his pipe while the dog takes a nap. A "dog's life" is a good life at Olga Bay.

Bill Pinnell stuffs a July 4 turkey.

No one ever goes hungry at Olga Bay.

Inside the Olga Bay "hotel"; one of the decaying structures located there.

Morris Tallifson constructing a new crab pot.

Morris Talifson plows a spud patch.

Unloading another year's grub supply.

Bill Pinnell, left, Morris Talifson, right.

men around the island also were allowed to keep theirs. But for the late-comers, there were not enough cabins to go around and the old-timers have been targets of green-eyed envy ever since.

"They call us 'that greedy P & T outfit' because we got here first," Pinnell explains. "The truth is, they're too soft to hunt out of tents!"

During the 1960's, jealousy was the rage of many who wanted to hunt out of P & T cabins. Resident hunters from Anchorage and nearby military bases naturally believed that the best areas were where the guides hunted. To a certain extent that theory was correct, but the myth that the biggest bears could only be found in P & T territory certainly was aided by the fact that such comfortable cabins existed there. Some local hunters actually began believing that they were being denied meaningful hunts because they were not allowed to force their way into P & T's cabins.

One spring, during the early 1970's, in a year when the winter had been extremely severe and six feet of snow still covered the south end of Kodiak, Bill Pinnell almost locked horns with the federal and state governments over his right to hunt out of his own cabin. In those days there wasn't any permit drawing system. The permits were simply issued on a first-come, first-served basis. For years P & T relied upon the help of a friend in town who stood in line and got permits for their hunters. Pinnell's friend was reliable and usually was the first person in line. But one year was different, because several local military hunters stood outside the refuge manager's door all night. They were ahead of Pinnell's friend when the refuge office opened the next morning. They asked for — and got — permits to hunt the south end of Karluk Lake, Pinnell's customary spring hunting area.

This predicament put Pinnell on the spot. He'd booked hunts for Karluk more than a year in advance. Now, he apparently would not be able to hunt out of his own cabin because some military "brass" had permits for that end of Karluk. Understandably concerned, Pinnell flew to town and met with the refuge manager.

"They said there wasn't anything they could do," Pinnell recalls. "So I asked the refuge manager where the other hunters intended to stay at Karluk (one of the men planned to bring his wife along). The manager took his red pen and pointed at a dot on his map that represented my cabin, and said with a funny little grin on his face, 'they might be planning to stay in the little shack right there.'

"'— — he will!' I exclaimed. I'll hire someone to stay in my cabin rather than allow someone else to use it! Besides, my hunters have been booked since last year, specifically to hunt Karluk. They'll sue me if I *don't* get the permits; so either way, I'll end up in court.'

"Then the assistant manager asked me, 'Who is your attorney?'

"So I told him, and he said, 'You're using a cannon to kill a mouse!'"

As the days crawled by, the entire P & T outfit sat in nervous anticipation of the situation's outcome. The spring bear season had almost arrived, and still no compromise had been reached. So Pinnell packed an outfit and headed for Karluk anyway, without hunting permits.

During the final days of the crisis, Pinnell's assistants did much speculating as to its outcome. P & T were not the lawless sorts. The pair had done as much as anyone to aid the cause of conserving and protecting Alaska's wildlife, and none doubted their intentions to continue doing so. But here was the principle of one being run out of his own camp after 20 years of guiding, and it being taken over by an outsider. Convinced of his right as a businessman, a right the territory and state had recognized up until now, Bill was determined to win, and he'd go down swinging in court if necessary.

With Pinnell entrenched at Karluk, the battle lines were well drawn. One assistant guide who was helping to set up another camp at Fraser Lake several days before open season remembers the appearance one morning of a large white Navy helicopter. It flew all through the country, over Fraser and around through Karluk Lake country. Snow obviously still was better than five feet deep at Karluk, and temperatures were well below freezing. Strangely enough, the very next day after that Navy helicopter made its tour over the country, Pinnell received a radio message from the Kodiak refuge manager, via Kodiak Airways. The assistant guide heard that, too.

"The other party decided not to hunt. You've got your permits, so go ahead and hunt."

When the next season rolled around, Pinnell and a hired man stood *two* days to be first in line for their permits. Pinnell continued this practice each season thereafter, until a more equitable permit drawing system was created.

A few years later, local refuge managers finally informed P & T that if they wanted their cabins to remain in Brown Bear country they would have to "dedicate" them to public use. Realizing that the writing was on the wall, P & T did this, but with the understanding that they would have "first use" of their own cabins whenever needed for clients. As a result, the P & T cabins became "public-use" cabins except during hunting season, or whenever needed by P & T for fishing parties, photographers, etc.

Since that time, the Interior Department has built a number of new public-use cabins on the refuge; these are situated so as to encourage hunters to distribute themselves more evenly. Most of these new structures still are located in the proximity of P & T hunting territory, however, and the result is that applicants for bear hunting permits in these areas are nine or ten times as numerous as in other areas. For all practical purposes, local hunters who continue insisting that "P & T territory is the only place to hunt" are wasting their efforts attempting to hunt there. Most of them never will get a chance to hunt there.

The spring sun rested a little higher on the horizon than it had the evening before when I struggled to the top of the moraine bluff above the beach. The silt gave way several times, and I almost fell before reaching the top. I was forced to remove my pack and shove it over the top before I could crawl over the edge onto a carpet of tundra moss. Exhausted, I sat gazing across endless waves stretching as far as my eyes could see. There was nothing to hear except rhythmic rolling waves pounding the beach, and occasional squeals from gulls. No wonder P & T speak so fondly of the life they knew as miners on this same beach so many years ago. I lamented the passing of yesteryears, and quietly began crossing the tundra to the head of Olga Bay.

CHAPTER XIV

I spent the night in "Danialson's cabin" at the head of Olga Bay. Built during the Great Depression by the miner whose name it still bears, this frame structure has survived countless gales. Yet, it remains solid. P & T bought the cabin from Danialson when the old fellow retired and moved to the pioneer's home back in the 1960's The two guides seldom used the cabin, but their packers and assistant guides often stayed there while trapping. When the Alaska Native Claims Settlement Act was passed, the cabin changed hands again. This time it was "claimed" by a local Native. Although lacking routine maintenance, the building remains sound, and provided the comfort I needed for a single night's rest.

The next day, I was able to visit another cabin. This one holds many memories for me. The cabin is located next to the lagoon at Silver Salmon Lake on Olga Bay's north shore. I left Danialson's cabin early because I wanted to spend some time at Silver Salmon before pressing on to the cannery. The beach was clean at low tide, which enabled me to make good time. I arrived at Silver Salmon a little before noon.

Silver Salmon will always be a special place for me. At the age of 18, I spent a great deal of time trapping there. The Silver Salmon "cabin" really is nothing more than a hut, or semi-barabara. Its superiority to a tent is debatable. But I used its shelter, and took advantage of each stay there as an occasion for developing my sense of self-reliance and knowledge of woodcraft. This structure was built by a native trapper during the 1930's. Its exterior sod embankments already were pushing its plank walls inward during my first winter there. Several boards in its floor had sprung loose making the room hazardous, and its door was hanging loosely by one badly rusted hinge. There were open holes all along the walls beneath the eaves which permitted cold wind to whistle about my ears at night. Any heat that I managed to generate in the cabin easily escaped through its tin roof. My one-burner camp stove never broke the chill. I nearly froze to death before morning. Yet I loved the place, hated to leave, and have always longed to return.

One of the reasons for my fondness of the little sod hut is the fact that I enjoyed a deeply spiritual experience there. I carried a Bible with me on each trip and spent hours reading it by candlelight before turning in each night. The prayer time I enjoyed there also gave me a great sense of nearness to God and implanted in me a better sense of purpose and direction for my life. I shall always be thankful for the time that I spent alone at Silver Salmon.

Compared with the spiritual feast I enjoyed, my physical existence at Silver Salmon was spartan. Not only was the cabin damp and cold, I also learned ways to make do with whatever was handy when a need arose. I found myself fashioning tools and utensils from scraps of wood, metal, or alder strips, and learned to eat the "boiled" fare that most far north trappers and explorers once ate. My meals usually consisted of boiled rice, cracked wheat, bacon, etc., with hot tea, and I sampled a variety of ducks and songbirds. I even ate part of a fox. The experience was good for me. It taught me that man is capable of living well with a lot less than most men today think they must have in order to survive.

The Silver Salmon cabin had changed little during the years of my absence. The door was flat on the ground by now, and the spring-boards in the floor were worse.

Someone had attempted to "modernize" the facilities by installing a moldy mattress on the hardboard bunk. The local weasel committee apparently had a great time pulling the mattress apart and scattering balls of cotton everywhere. Surprisingly, a coffee can stash of food that I left behind years before still was covered with its plastic lid, and the goodies still were there too.

Because Silver Salmon only is about three or four hours from the Olga Bay cannery, I knew I could reach it by late evening. The tide already was rising, however, so I had to hurry. If the tide was too high, I wouldn't be able to wade past rock cliffs along the beach.

The sun was below the horizon when I rounded the last point of beach and viewed Olga Bay cannery that evening. The sound of P & T's gasoline generator droned across flat sea water before I caught sight of dim light. Otherwise, the camp was silent as I trudged up the boardwalk. Morris Talifson's gasoline lantern shown through his window when I clumped past; I saw the elder guide sitting at his desk doing book work with a calculator. He nodded and smiled as I passed. I felt gratified by my excursion through Brown Bear country as I retired in the "hunter's quarters" that night. I tried hard to recall a more enjoyable occasion, but found solace in the realization that all of my outings on Kodiak had been just that — enjoyable.

Bill Pinnell was occupying his captain's chair when I strolled through the door the next morning. He perked up a bit when I entered.

"You returned just in time!" he declared with a grin. "We're about to plant the garden and we need all the help we can get!"

The ground was thoroughly warm now. Talifson had his rototiller fine-tuned. In fact, he had already broken ground for a brand new garden plot next to the hunters' quarters. Before the crew could begin planting potatoes, however, one final "bear hunting" chore remained to be done. The bear hides that had been nailed to the hide house floor were well cured now and needed to be readied for shipment to taxidermists.

P & T probably have shipped bear hides to more taxidermists than any two bear guides alive. Over the years, P & T have developed tastes and opinions regarding the work of several taxidermists, too. Bill Pinnell respects the work of most, but never has stopped laughing at one taxidermist who mounted a bear's hind feet on its front legs. He also scorns some taxidermists who promote life-size mounted bears with "silly snarls."

"Those bears look ridiculous," Pinnell says. "Bears don't snarl and lurch about like that in real life!"

Few guides go to the effort that P & T go to in preparing bear hides for shipment. Talifson is a perfectionist, and his experience as a fur farmer and fur buyer compels him to do so. Each hide was shaken almost clean of salt, then draped over a long pole, and hauled out of the hide house to hang in open air. There they remained for a day or two, until all remaining moisture had gone from the fur.

Several of the big skins sported fair-sized "rubs," but most were surprisingly free of such defects. The guides here are well instructed about the necessity of looking over each animal before the hunter downs it to make sure there aren't any bad rubs. Only if a client's hunt is almost ended is he advised to shoot a rubbed bear. These precautions aren't taken because there is any shame in downing a rubbed bear, but because such a bear should be allowed to grow a better coat before being harvested, if possible.

As soon as Talifson was certain that each trophy was free of moisture, it was bundled inside a large, heavy-duty canvas shipping bag. These bags are virtually air-tight, except at their tops, and are provided by various taxidermists. Each hide was tagged with a card identifying the hunter and giving his mounting instructions. Each bundle also was tagged with an official Alaska export permit as required by law. The elder guide's work being complete, he could finally relax and wait for the hides to depart on the next available flight.

Very few P & T hunters ever have complained about the treatment that their hides have received after leaving Olga Bay. The reason probably is that P & T have such a strong reputation across the nation that most taxidermists are eager to gain their approval; they try harder to do a good job on any trophy received through P & T. This has not always been the case, however.

One young P & T hunter took a beautiful Kodiak Brown Bear trophy and, against Bill Pinnell's advice, sent it to a particular firm for preparation. Months later, the young hunter was disappointed to receive shipment of a *Black* Bear. Although the young man protested, the proprietor never admitted that a "mistake" had been made. Apparently this man didn't know that Black Bears do not inhabit Kodiak Island.

When Bill Pinnell heard that the young hunter's trophy had landed in someone else's jackpot, he allowed the man to return for a second hunt, free of charge. But this hunter failed to score on the second hunt, although he did mortally wound a bear that escaped. To my knowledge, the man has never taken another bear. He told me, "I've killed two bears — I don't feel that I've got the right to kill another one any time soon." This hunter later worked for P & T as an assistant guide and eventually earned a full guide's license.

Stories like this one are common. Even a federal Fish and Wildlife agent of long standing in Alaska admitted to me that he was victimized by a crooked taxidermist years ago. He lost a good Brown Bear trophy in a raw deal. But big bear hunters aren't the only victims. Virtually any valuable big game trophy is a potential tartget for theft.

A retired Marine colonel I know sent a beautiful Dall sheep cape to be mounted by a large firm. The taxidermist wrote him months later, and told him that his cape wasn't worth mounting because most of its hair had slipped in tanning. Alarmed, the colonel asked the taxidermist to send the cape to him for inspection. He had shot his sheep square in the neck, but when the cape arrived there wasn't a bullet hole anywhere in it. The colonel protested that his sheep had somehow gotten switched, but according to the taxidermist, such a "mistake" was impossible. The taxidermist argued that because he places his *own* identification on each hide he receives, no hide could possibly get switched. The colonel finally threw up his hands in disgust — so to speak — and later declared himself to be a wiser man as a result of his unfortunate experience.

Some taxidermists will admit that they switch hides. One taxidermist told me, "...It's a common practice for taxidermists to replace skins that they lose or ruin with others they have gotten elsewhere... [Taxidermists usually go] to a lot of trouble to find [replacement skins]. So why should [the hunter] want to sue [them.]" This man didn't realize that a true hunter wants his *own* trophy — not someone else's.

Another taxidermist confessed, "...No taxidermist can survive without extra hides to use for replacements and patchwork. That's why I buy every hide I can get my hands on!"

Therefore, some hides apparently get switched by taxidermists with self-declared altruistic motives. However, another reason why some hides get switched by taxidermists and tanners may be *profit*. Brown Bear rugs often are advertised for sale in the want-ad sections of publications like the *Wall Street Journal,* at prices ranging from $10,000 to $15,000. Most of these hides undoubtedly come from honest sellers, but their published worth is demonstrative of value. A taxidermist I am acquainted with liquidated a Brown Bear rug from an estate for $13,300. Nice Brown Bear hides are valuable.

Conversely, poor quality Brown Bear hides are cheap. The Alaska Department of Fish and Game holds auctions for the sale of hides. Most of these are taken from nuisance bears and animals killed in defense of life or property. Many of these bruins are killed during the summer when bears are plentiful but poorly furred. Some are clearly trash hides and can be purchased for just a fraction of what a fine October or November skin would cost. Other cheap skins can be bought at raw fur auctions, most notably in Canada and in the Soviet Union. But the cheapest source of "extra" hides for shady taxidermists or tanners would be poachers operating in Alaska and elsewhere. Crooked taxidermists and tanners can profitably switch the prime October and November trophies belonging to their customers with cheap summer skins picked up at auction or bought from poachers for a few hundred dollars each. Just a few such capers can generate enormous revenues for the individual involved in this illicit trade.

I once had a candid conversation on this topic with a man who had worked several years for one of Alaska's more notorious "bandit" guides. I asked him how the crooked taxidermists and tanners were able to filter illegal hides in and out of their tanneries and shops without being detected by federal Fish and Wildlife officers who occasionally inspect them. With a twinkle in his eyes, he said, ". . . That's just one of the mysteries of life, I guess."

Nevertheless, reports of switched trophies are so common that one Alaska Fish and Game official wrote, ". . . There seem to be complaints every year that bear hides are being switched by various taxidermists. . .; [it's about time that something is done about it]."

Unfortunately, there isn't much that can be done about this problem, and no one is more aware of that fact than the taxidermists and tanners who switch hides. A few years ago, a friend of mine visited an established furrier in an attempt to gather information on a case of suspected bear hide switching. The furrier was very friendly, but politely declared that crooked taxidermists and tanners are virtually immune from detection.

"[The hunter] can't prove that the hide was switched," he said.

"Why not?"

"Because they will say the [the hunter] didn't know how to skin [his] bear."

202

"But [the hunter] *did* know how to skin [his] bear!"

"Then, they will say that [the hunter] let his hide rot, or that some defect in the hide caused it to look different after tanning!"

The furrier continued, and explained how he had been cheated on several occasions by crooked tanneries. On two separate occasions he sent wolf skins to be tanned by a particular tannery. The first time, he sent a fine quality skin, but received a smaller, poor quality skin of a different color in return. The second time, he sent a cheap hide like the one the tanner had returned to him the first time; but this time the tanner sent him a beautiful large skin in return.

In another case, this furrier sent 100 prime Alaskan red fox skins to be tanned, but he received a shipment of cheap east coast foxes in return. Experienced furriers can identify the approximate origin of furs by color and quality. Regardless of the fact that this man was dealt a crooked hand in each incident he related, he didn't press a single claim. Apparently, this is a hazard of the trade that some furriers accept as a cost of doing business.

In spite of the furrier's unwillingness to press his rightful claims, he did know what he was talking about when he outlined the basic arguments that can be made by any taxidermist or tanner who is accused of switching bear hides. Of course, not every accused taxidermist or tanner is guilty in every instance. But by carefully considering these arguments, one can easily see why crooked taxidermists and tanners are so difficult to prosecute.

In the first place, proving just *who* switched a hide is complicated by the number of times that a hide changes hands in the normal process of tanning and mounting. After the bear hunter departs, his guide sends the hide to the taxidermist, sometimes through a third party known as a "receiving agent." After the taxidermist gets the hide, which may be five or six weeks later, he usually forwards it again, this time to a tannery. Then, several months later, the hide is returned to the taxidermist who ships a trophy to the hunter, who may or may not appreciate what he receives. After the hide has changed hands five or six times, it's rather difficult to determine just "who done it."

If the hunter believes that his hide was switched by someone in particular, that individual can simply deny any wrongdoing. He can passively pass the buck on the other parties involved by saying "I didn't do it, but if it was done, then the others did it." All of the parties, however, recognize their interdependence in the dispute. All have an interest in preventing the hunter from proving that the switch actually occured. If the hunter can't prove that, then no one will be blamed for it. Even the innonent parties will be afraid of getting the blame. Furthermore, long-standing business relationships may provide a catalyst for unity, even if the hide obviously was switched. Therefore, all of the suspects concentrate their efforts on disproving that the hunter's trophy was switched.

When the hunter's trophy merely has been switched with a smaller hide, the hunter has the hardest of all cases to prove. Hides normally shrink about 10 percent in tanning. Hunters frequently are surprised by the smaller size. So, the taxidermist or tanner explains this fact, and adds that "It's just another case of an overly excited bear hunter thinking that his bruin was a whole lot bigger than it really was." The hunter is made to sound like the fisherman with a big fish that got away. Most neutral third parties, and quite often the hunter himself, can be convinced that the right hide was returned, even if it wasn't.

The arguments are more sophisticated, and confusing, when a high-quality trophy has been switched with a poor skin. This is where the arguments outlined by the furrier earlier in this chapter come into play. Most taxidermists and tanners include in their contracts and literature standard disclaimer clauses referred to by lawyers as "boiler-plate." These are called "boilerplate" because theoretically they "cover all bases" and provide the party hiding behind them with "ironclad" protection. The wording may vary, but these disclaimers ordinarily contain two very important provisions for taxidermists and tanners. One provision usually alleges, in essence, that because the taxidermist or tanner has no control over the manner in which a hide is handled prior to his receipt, he can't be held responsible for bad results caused by improper handling. The other provision ordinarily alleges in essence, that hides and skins are subject to innumerable, unknown, hidden, and totally unexplainable defects that cannot be detected before tanning; therefore, if a hide doesn't fare well in tanning, then it's the fault of one of those defects and not that of the taxidermist or tanner.

These provisions sound reasonable in themselves. Most taxidermists and tanners who use them are honest and sincere, and are well advised to do so. If I were a taxidermist or tanner, I would use boilerplate provisions in all of my contracts and literature. However, these two provisions allow crooked taxidermists and tanners to shift responsibility for just about anything. Both give rise to arguments which can be used to explain away any differences between the hunter's real trophy and the hide that he receives from the taxidermist or tanner. And in order to overcome either, the hunter needs a lot more evidence than a few casual snapshots and testimony from a hunting buddy.

If the taxidermist or tanner has switched the real trophy with a hide exhibiting evidence of improper handling prior to tanning, then the provision pertaining to that problem comes into play. The taxidermist or tanner argues that he didn't switch hides, that the hunter got his own hide, and that it looks the way it does because the hunter did not treat it properly prior to receipt by the taxidermist or tanner. This not only *multiplies* the burden of proof that the hunter must meet, as will be explained shortly, but in many cases it effectively places the hunter himself on trial. This situation is analogous to that of a girl who must prove that she was a virgin before her assailant will be convicted of rape. In order to prove that the taxidermist or tanner switched his hide, the hunter must first prove that he provided ideal care for his trophy at all times. However, because of the peculiar process of properly caring for a hide, this burden of proof may be impossible to meet, regardless of the fine care that a hide has received.

The hunter who seeks to prove that he properly handled his trophy usually must address problem areas on the hide which are affected by "slippage." Improperly treated hides usually exhibit areas of slippage. Slippage occurs during tanning when entire areas of hair or fur fall out, or "slip" from the hide, leaving behind bald patches of leather. The taxidermist may or may not patch these slipped areas with patches of hide from another bear.

Slippage ordinarily has two causes. It can be caused if the hunter, guide, or receiving agent fleshes the hide too close, thus cutting into the roots of hair or fur. Because the roots are severed, nothing is left to hold the hair or fur in place; so it slips out of the hide during tanning, leaving behind bald leather.

Slippage is also caused by tainting. If the hunter doesn't flesh and salt his trophy in a timely fashion, or is unable to keep it adequately cooled until it is fleshed and salted, the hide may taint. If a hide taints, its fur will slip out of it during tanning anywhere it is affected by taint, leaving behind bald leather. Therefore, if the hide exhibits evidence of slippage, the hunter is faced with a real "catch-22." He can be accused of mishandling his own hide, even if he properly fleshed and salted it in the field.

In most cases, the hunter must be able to prove that his own hide received the finest care. The hunter must do this in order to rebut the claim that the hide in dispute looks different because he mishandled it. Unfortunately, most hunters leave the field without nearly enough documentation to meet this burden. Sometimes circumstances beyond a hunter's control create a scenario from which inferences can be drawn that the hide *might have* tainted in spite of proper handling by the hunter.

In situations where the hunter happens to have sufficient evidence that he properly treated his trophy, the second "boilerplate" disclaimer provision dealing with mysterious hidden defects can swing into play. Here, the taxidermist or tanner argues that he didn't switch the hide, that hides can go bad in tanning because of unknown, unnamed, and totally unexplainable hidden defects, and that any change of appearance about the hide resulted from such a defect.

Because no one can say for sure just what the defect really was, the taxidermist or tanner can use this argument to explain away anything he wants to explain away about a hide. The hide may exhibit "slipped" areas, or it may have fallen apart in tanning. It may continually shed fur after tanning, just like a molting dog, or it may have lost all of its guardhairs and have only its underfur left. The hide may not even be the same color. But regardless of the problem, the taxidermist or tanner can blame it on a "hidden defect."

The idea of blaming anything and everything that can go wrong with a hide on a hidden defect would seem ridiculous except for the fact that it is arguable. The hunter cannot prove the non-existence of the defect any more than the taxidermist or tanner can prove its existence. No one can prove with certainty the existence or non-existence of something that has never before been seen or identified. However, the taxidermist or tanner doesn't have to identify the defect. He simply says, "I don't know why perfectly good hides fall apart, or do this, or that, during tanning, but every so often they do it. Therefore, some defect must cause it!"

When that statement is made by a person who has tanned thousands of hides, and has years of experience under his belt, how can the hunter refute it? He may not be able to. Because the taxidermist or tanner is an "expert" in the field, any prudent expert from outside the field will defer to his opinion; and other "expert" taxidermists or tanners may decline to dispute the issue if they also allege "hidden defects" in their own boilerplate disclaimers.

If there ever was a subject in need of practical scientific clarification, it is this matter of hidden defects. Although the science of tanning has been with man for thousands of years, it is rather mysterious to a lot of people today. Defects may indeed afflict some hides, and honest taxidermists and tanners certainly shouldn't be held liable for the results when that is the case. But this writer suspects that sufficient research and testing could reveal that most, if not almost all, of the alleged "hidden defects" exist only in the minds of their advocates; their "mental existence" may sometimes be encouraged by a burning desire to beat charges of hide switching or negligence in tanning. Perhaps someday, an *independent* scientific authority will strip taxidermists and tanners of their self-proclaimed expertise on "hidden defects" in game animal hides.

In spite of diverting arguments that can be raised, there are some basic, but very important, points that should be remembered when distinguishing between hides.

First, there is more than one way to skin a bear. Most hunters and guides skin their animals by extending the belly cut from the bear's throat all the way to the base of its tail. Then, when the rear leg cuts are extended from the tail's base, the skinned hide is given a contoured shape along its bottom edge. This contour on each side of the hide's tail will closely match the shape of the rear side of each hind leg.

If, on the other hand, the belly cut is stopped six or eight inches up the belly from the base of the tail, and each hind leg cut is extended straight out to the hind foot from the end of the belly cut, the bottom edge of the hide will be straight across. By skinning the bear this way, its hide is given a "square" appearance, and its length is increased. Few hunters realize that skinning a bear this way will make it look larger and actually improve its appearance. However, some guides regularly practice this method, which is accepted as proper throughout the industry.

The point is, that if the hunter's bear was skinned one way, but he receives a hide that was skinned the other way, he can be confident that someone in the chain of custody switched his hide. After a hide has been skinned one way, no one can alter the fact by making it appear that it was skinned the other way. If a bear was skinned with a "square" tail end, then skin that would have been attached along each side above the hind legs will be at the bottom edge instead. Conversely, if the hide is skinned with a contoured rear end, then the skin that would have been at the bottom edge will be attached above each hind leg along the flank.

No one can undo these basic cuts without rearranging some skin and leaving behind stitches to prove it. A "square" skinned hide can be trimmed so that its bottom edge will match that of a "contoured" hide, but there won't be as much hide above the hind legs as there would have been if it had been skinned that way, unless someone sews it back on. So the difference still will be apparent. A diagram, showing how the hide has been skinned, should be prepared before the hide is turned over to a taxidermist or tanner, and the taxidermist or tanner should be required to sign it, too.

Another more frequent distinction among hides is rubs. Rubs are places on the bear's hide where its pile of fur has been worn short. Usually, rubs are caused by rubbing, but they also occur in the den when fur freezes to the earth and the animal then moves about, causing its hair to be broken off. There are about as many configurations of rubs among bears as there are fingerprints among humans. A hide may be rubbed on its rump, along its flanks, on the side of its legs, or on the fronts of its paws. It may have one rub, or it may have many, located in any combination of places.

Extensive research by Fish and Game authorities in Alaska has proven that as many as 50 percent of all Brown Bear killed in the spring are rubbed, whereas only about nine percent are rubbed in the fall. Bears taken in the spring also are more likely to be badly rubbed, as opposed to fall bears which tend to be rubbed only slightly, if at all.

The reason for this is simple. Each year the bear puts on a fresh coat of fur — just like a dog does. As mentioned, a Brown Bear may already sport noticeable rubs when it leaves its den. But, after consuming most of the nutrients stored in its body for winter survival, a bear's coat of fur is drained of much of its vitality and luster. Then, as the weather warms, the animal no longer needs the warmth of a heavy coat, so it begins shedding. The shedding process is aided by the fact that warmer weather brings insects and discomfort beneath the heavy coat, and the bear begins rubbing hither and thither to relieve itself. The result is that large patches of longer fur begin disappearing from the bear's body. In fact, as the fur departs, big wads of ugly, matted fur form and these hang and dangle from the bear's body in rag-tag fashion. The process is similar to that which can be observed among long-haired dogs in northern regions.

A bear shot in this condition is sometimes likened unto a "poodle dog," because of the patches of very short fur interspersed amidst long fur. Taxidermists can trim the fur surrounding rubs so that the rubs aren't quite so bold, but most badly rubbed spring hides remain less than impressive on trophy room walls. This is why guides carefully examine bears for rubs before letting clients shoot them.

By June, most Brown Bears are very badly rubbed. The shedding process continues all summer until all of the old fur has shed and the animals are covered with new coats of short, healthy fur. Because this new, short fur is cleaner and cooler, the bear is less inclined to rub aginst rocks or trees to relieve itch. Also, the bear gorges itself each summer on rich, oily salmon. This diet produces vibrant, lustrous, and durable new growth. By mid-October, Brown Bears are covered with full coats of fur; this fur is practically as long as it ever will get, although slight growth continues while the animal's body functions are slowed by hibernation. The bear's fur needs to be well developed before denning if the beast is to survive the winter. The result of this annual schedule is a beautiful, evenly furred, fall bear, void of any serious rubs, if it is rubbed at all.

Many hunters have heard taxidermists and tanners declare, "Spring is when you get the best hides. Fall hides are all rubbed." That statement simply isn't true. Years ago, hunters were allowed to kill Brown Bears from September 1 until June 20. Perhaps one could say that a bear killed on September 1 is "rubbed" if the new coat of fur it sports is very short, as it would be. But today, Brown Bear season on most of Kodiak does not begin until October 25, and by then the bear's new coat of fur is fully developed.

The location of rubs on a hide may indicate the time of year it was taken. Fall rubs usually are located in the flank areas where the bear contacts brush, etc., when walking. Spring rubs may be anywhere on the animal, particularly in those areas where fur ordinarily is deepest and thickest, such as the middle of the animal's back and top of its shoulders. A spring bear often starts rubbing in the rump area before it does elsewhere. A spring bear also is often rubbed on the top sides of its paws as a result of walking through hard, crusty snow.

Taxidermists and tanners sometimes argue that rubs go unnoticed until after tanning. They argue that the bear, being a "big dirty beast," often is covered with matted fur, etc., that doesn't come loose until tanning. Then after tanning, the rub finally can be seen. This argument is completely self-serving, because no one but the taxidermist or tanner is around to see whether additional rubs appear during tanning. The kind of wads of matted fur exhibited on spring hides seldom, if ever, exist on fall hides. Even when such wads of matted fur do occur, they are clearly visible and easily shaken or pulled from the hide. Any guide who has skinned and shaken the hides of a dozen bears knows that rubs are clearly visible *before* hides are shipped to taxidermists or tanners.

One guide told me, "The only way [a rub] can appear on a hide for the first time after tanning is if [the taxidermist or tanner] does a lot of 'rubbing' on it himself!"

In any event, the hunter should note on a diagram the exact shape, location, and extent, of any rubs on his bear before releasing it to a taxidermist or tanner. The taxidermist or tanner should be required to sign this diagram, too.

Taxidermists and tanners sometimes argue that a hunter's fall hide wasn't "prime," and that this is why the hide he received has an unseemly appearance. A hide is prime if it has a well-developed coat of underfur. It is unprime if it does not. The flesh side of a hide with an under-developed coat of underfur will turn blue when dried, whereas that of a hide with well-developed underfur usually will remain white or creamy-colored when dried. Furriers often identify unprime raw hides by the bluish skin they sport. However, unprime hides tan just as nicely as prime hides; they simply lack a real heavy coat of underfur. As previously stated, Brown Bears have well-developed coats of underfur my mid-October, and therefore are prime.

The color of a hide's fur may indicate the time of year it was taken. Because of a rich salmon diet, and fewer hours of sunshine in the fall, a fall Brown Bear tends to have a much darker coat than its spring counterpart. After consuming most of the nutrients stored in its body for winter survival, a spring bear's coat is coarser and drained of its vitality and luster. This phenomenon can be observed in other furbearers, too. Witness the "cherry red" color of the fall red fox. By spring, its fur is coarser, paler, and less valuable. Furriers know the difference and adjust their prices accordingly. Furthermore, after a bear leaves its den, it usually is subjected to weeks of almost continuous sunshine reflected off snow. This sunlight will bleach the fur to even lighter tones than it had upon leaving the den.

The color of claws can also distinguish hides. A younger bear will have dark claws, but as it grows older, its claws become creamy colored and eventually white. A Brown Bear ordinarily has white claws by age 10. Another point to remember is that bears under three years of age have a ring of creamy white fur around their shoulders and neck.

No hunter should ever relinquish custody of a valuable Brown Bear hide without first securing adequate proof of identity. Fish and Game tags are easily removed and placed on different hides, and the hunter shouldn't rely upon his taxidermist's or tanner's identification system to prove which hide is his own. However, the hunter needs some sort of positive identification to distinguish his own trophy from others just like it.

Some hunters I know place marks on claws, or punch holes in their hides. These should be closely photographed. No such method is entirely fool proof because such marks can be duplicated. This writer has thought of at least two means of identifying Brown Bear hides that *might* work. First, he can "fingerprint" the toe pads on his bear hide the same way police fingerprint humans. Why should patterns of bear toes be any more common than those of human fingers? Hopefully, Fish and Game biologists will someday confirm this. Secondly, the hunter can weld a good-sized stainless steel ring onto his hide, preferably near the center of the hide, between its shoulders, where it will be out of the way. Attach an identification tag to the ring and have *the weld x-rayed*. No two welds are the same. If the ring is removed and replaced on another hide, the hunter will have evidence of the fact. The hunter should make the taxidermist or tanner agree *in writing* that this ring will not be removed until the hide is returned to the hunter. A taxidermist or tanner may later claim that the ring was accidentally removed, but if serious questions arise concerning the identity of the trophy, he won't look very good by saying so.

A hunter should thoroughly document his hunt. The first thing he should do in camp is establish a weather log and record wind, temperature and precipitation daily. Then, if the taxidermist or tanner argues that his hide rotted in a sauna, he can pull out his records to prove temperature, etc. This is particularly important in areas where seasons still open in September.

As soon as the bear is dead, the hunter should log the time, and start his camera clicking. He should photograph the skinning process in detail, to have proof of each cut in the hide, expecially those near the hind end. If the hide is skinned "square," good pictures are needed to show how it was done. Log the time when the skinning is complete.

The hunter also should photograph the hide cooling in open air before it is bundled for packing. He should log the air temperature and length of time allowed for cooling. He should also photograph the hide being fleshed; he should log the time that fleshing starts and the time that it is finished. The hunter should photograph the fleshed side of the hide at close range, to demonstrate that no fat was left on the hide. But he should remember that a crooked taxidermist or tanner still can argue that the hide was fleshed "too close."

Then, the hunter should photograph both sides of the bear hide at close range to document all rubs, if any, and the exact location of bullet holes. He should have handy, a large, coarse comb, and should photograph the fur being combed in "search" of so-called "hidden rubs."

The hunter ought to log the exact time that salt is applied to the fleshed hide, as well as the amount of salt applied (by weight). Remember, a half-pound of non-iodized salt is required for each pound of hide. Photographs should be taken of the salting taking place and of the empty containers arranged so that they can be counted.

If the salted hide is to be stored for a few days, its location should be photographed to demonstrate that it was not left in direct sunlight. Thermometers should be posted and regular readings should be recorded.

Finally, the hunter should ask his guide to sign a written statement, describing the hide *in detail* from head to tail, and making note of its condition. Then, if the hunter delivers the hide directly to the taxidermist or tanner, he should pull out that statement, and present it to the person with whom he does business. The taxidermist or tanner should be asked to sign the statement, and to personally declare in writing whether the hide exhibits any sign of execessive fleshings, tainting or rubs. If the taxidermist or tanner won't sign such a statement, then the hunter should consider whether he wants to do business with him. The hunter has as much of a right to protect his own interests, as the taxidermist or tanner has to do business. He shouldn't be buffaloed if someone wants to hassle him about these precautions. The hide he saves may be his own.

All of these precautions may seem burdensome to many hunters. The author certainly believes that hunts should be enjoyed. But he also believes that *memories* of a hunt should be enjoyed, too. A crooked taxidermist or tanner robs the hunter of those memories the moment he steals the hide. The hide is a momento that symbolizes the hunt. Bitter memories of a stolen hide greatly diminish the hunter's joy when he recalls the event. A Brown Bear trophy has intrinsic value to the hunter who took it. This intrinsic value greatly exceeds the market value of fine trophies. Therefore, an ounce of prevention is worth more than a pound of cure. If the taxidermist or tanner *knows* that the hunter is alert, hopefully he won't be tempted to steal the prize. But if a crooked taxidermist or tanner does steal the hunter's trophy, then the hunter may be able to prove it, and make him pay the full price.

CHAPTER XV

As soon as the hunter's trophies were shipped to various taxidermists, the P & T crew turned its attention to annual summertime chores. The ground was thoroughly warm now. Talifson had his rototiller fine tuned. And the next annual chore was the garden.

P & T always have gardens; they grow a surprising variety of produce. Bears in the raspberries are common occurrences. Of course, some vegetables are grown in a greenhouse. But the guides never lack fresh vegetables when these items are in season.

After breakfast, everyone donned hip-boots, picked up tools and sacks of seed potatoes, and started up the boardwalk toward the "upper" garden on the other side of Akalura Creek. The creek is very shallow there, and three of us struggled to tote the rototiller across.

"Last year we lost a lot of spuds in the upper garden to a nuisance bear." Talifson remarked.

There still were old bear tracks in the mud to prove that a bruin had frequented this patch. In fact, the bear had left behind a ditch where he uprooted spuds.

The soil on Kodiak's south end is, of course, quite stoney. Consequently, at harvest it sometimes is difficult to tell rocks from spuds. But the soil is rich, dark, and deep. Even though most of the potatoes are no bigger than silver dollars, they are sweet.

"We eat them like apples!" Pinnell brags.

So do some of his friends in town. Pinnell sometimes sends parcels of potatoes to select individuals of long acquaintance. Those friends are depended upon by P & T to run occasional errands that the guides need taken care of while they are isolated in the bush. The recipients appreciate the potatoes, and P & T appreciate their services.

After tilling, raking, and planting the upper garden, the crew returned to the cannery and did the same to three more plots. By the end of the day, all the P & T gardens were planted.

"Some years we only get a few hundred pounds, but in a good season we harvest two to three thousand pounds," says Pinnell. "And our greenhouse yields other fresh vegetables, to boot."

As soon as the gardens were planted, another supply of food — ready to eat — was at the doorstep. The crew was washing dishes the next morning when a packer announced that he could hear a boat coming. Sure enough, a light-blue purse-seiner was approaching from the south. It hauled several thousand pounds of grub.

The guides receive groceries each June. By the time it arrives, the pantry has a few bare spots, and the packers are looking forward to new flavors. The crew sorted groceries as they were unloaded and hauled onto the dock. There were five or six kinds of canned vegetables, four or five varieties of canned soup, several flavors of jam, etc. There also were several cases of "Spam®." P & T are famous around the island for serving Spam® sandwiches.

When the boat was emptied, it floated noticeably higher, and the dock was cluttered with an immense variety of food. Several hours later, the goods were stored and the boat was out of sight. In a few days, the boat would return with an even heavier load of fuel oil and gasoline.

Independence and self-reliance characterizes the life-style at Olga Bay. Once supplied for the season, P & T have little need for the outside world. Consequently, life at Olga Bay remains tranquil and serene most of the year.

With seasonal chores accomplished, the P & T crew began diminishing for the summer. Several packers left to go to work as weir attendants, while one young man headed off to work at a cannery. As for me,

I engaged the two guides in bear hunting discussions. Soon I had both men outlining for me their secrets for success. Talifson began by explaining the dynamics of wind and the part that it plays on a Brown Bear hunt.

"In any hunting," he said, "*wind* is the most important element to consider. Knowing the direction of the wind and knowing how to get around the various currents is paramount. You can get into situations where you think you know the wind, but up in the canyons you'll discover currents that come in from different angles, scattering your scent in no telling how many different directions. I've had that happen lots of times, and lost some nice bears as a result."

"You can't see the wind, but as long as it is blowing strong enough, you can keep an eye on grass and leaves up ahead to tell the wind. While climbing up a mountain, you'll often find wind blowing opposite directions in alternate layers. This happened as we stalked one bear near the top of a hill. There was nothing I could do but go up through those currents, and I finally discovered that the last layer was blowing in the wrong direction. My only option then, was to move around, and come down on the bear from above. Well, when we got to the crest of the hill, I found that the real wind direction was cross-wise to all the other currents. Those alternating layers of air actually were wind currents blowing around both sides of the hill as the main wind was against the other side. We couldn't stalk the animal from that side, we had to go back below and wait for it to move off of the hill so we could get at it. When you climb a hill on the protected, down-wind side, you can expect alternating currents from both sides."

When one considers the many successful P & T Brown Bear hunts, and their tremendous record of collecting record-class trophies for their clients, one shouldn't be fooled by concluding that they bagged anywhere near the number of animals they actually stalked. An extreme example of how many bears they stalked for each bruin bagged, was the case when Bill Pinnell showed a world-famous hunter twenty-seven bears in a single day and failed to nail a single one.

"Seeing them, and gettin' up on them, are two different things," the oldtimer avers. "Almost anything can happen to spoil a perfect stalk."

Relighting his pipe, Morris rolled several large puffs, then continued to expound.

"There's no end to the variables of wind," says Morris. "You'll have different kinds of currents in different types of gullies and canyons. The wind currents and drafts often are different directions. It will blow around the hill from both sides. One time the wind will blow up the hill from one side, and a little while later it might blow down or around the hill from the other side. By staying right up on that point, they're safe, and unless you get lucky, you probably won't even get up to him. I've had that happen, and when they're smart enough to figure that out, you've got problems."

Hand in hand with wind, goes the dilemma of smoke from cigarettes and other forms of tobacco.

"They can smell that smoke a lot farther than they can smell a human," says Talifson. "And too, somebody might have been in the country smoking cigarettes all along, and the bears have gotten used to it. But let someone come in and start smoking cigars, or a pipe, and that is a foreign odor. They'll be wary of the unfamiliar smell. I smoke a pipe, and I've taken out hunters who smoked cigars, or even another brand of pipe tobacco, and when the bears smelled that, it was something new."

"Smoke from a camp woodstove also can be bad. All our cabins have woodstoves, but we try not to use them if it isn't necessary. Trouble is, when you've got a camp full of hunters to feed, and it's cold, sometimes you can't get away from using a woodstove. Such smoke disturbs a lot of bears, so I know it isn't the best thing in the world. But we usually wind up using the wood stove anyway. After we've been in camp a few days, the bears seem to get used to our smoke."

Talifson admits that he's encountered many difficult situations while stalking bears and trying to overcome the various currents of air. But the biggest problem, he says, occurs when you stalk a bear on a hillside, and while you're trying to keep out of sight and get into a favorable downwind position on the way up, the animal moves from where you figured it would be.

"You might get up there," he asserts, "and discover the bear has moved. And before you can find the animal again, it might move over and run into your tracks where you went up the hill and find out that you're right close. Then you've lost it."

"I had that happen with a packer year ago last spring, but he was

218

just going too fast. He went around up above a bunch of brush, and if the bear had stayed put he would have come out just right. But while my packer was going through the brush and around the top, the bear came down on the other side and went underneath the brush. He couldn't see the bear, yet the animal got over and ran into the hunter's tracks!''

"We try not to move around in an area for at least two weeks before we hunt. Tracking up the countryside can be detrimental to successful Brown Bear hunting. I've sat and watched bears bolt off and run after coming across our tracks. But, like every other facet of bear hunting, a bear's reaction to human tracks is variable as well. Sometimes, human tracks won't bother a bear at all. I've had bears come across our tracks and start following us. It all depends upon how many people the animals are used to, and how heavily they've been hunted. If they're accustomed to a lot of people, like during the summer months, bears won't be alarmed when they find human tracks. Or, if bears aren't used to being hunted heavily, the animals might not be afraid. There's no set rule.''

Besides wind, and the Brown Bear's use of smell, a bear's sight is the next most important factor that hunters must consider.

"Brown Bears don't depend on their sight,'' declares Talifson. "But never forget that they can see quite well. Generally, bears won't use their eyes unless spooked, and then they will watch you. But I've been out on the lake ice in the spring — like over at Fraser where bears have been hunted heavily in the spring, and are spooky — and have had them spot me almost from the tops of mountains. They'd see us out on the ice and take off. And in the fall, I also have had them spot me when I was out in the boat. The bears would smell or hear us, and then spot us in the boat, and just lie down on the beach and watch us. I've had an awful time trying to figure out how to get around some of those bears. The bears are getting smarter. A lot smarter!''

As a prime example of the Brown Bear's reliance on its eyesight, and how it can affect a hunt, Talifson recalls one of the earlier spring hunts of his career.

"We took two hunters to Fraser Lake,'' he remembers. "We walked over there from the cannery in those days. The morning after we got there, we started to go down to the lake, and one of the hunters had left his camera at the cabin; so I turned around and went back to get it for him. While I was going back to the cabin, Bill spotted what looked like an eagle sitting up on the hill behind the cabin. So he watched it, and pretty soon there were two of them. Then Bill looked through his binoculars, and there it was — a bear lying on a knoll right back up behind camp.''

"So then the bear stood up, and we went on up towards it after it had started moving. We got up there and the bear had headed away from it's spot under the alder brush. We were up on a ridge, and the bear broke out of the alders — oh — quite a ways from us; but then it *spotted* us. Well, we just stood there, and the bear turned around and came back under the alder brush. It was going to sneak around to see what we were — you know, smell of us. We went back and caught it just as it was coming around the edge of the brush. The hunter was using .375's with silvertip bullets, and he had to shoot the bear nine times to kill it. One the ninth shot, he finished the bear off. When the bear finally expired, it rolled down the hill onto the lake.''

"The next day, we went up the lake, and got up on a ridge to glass across the ice. There was another bear that had come out of about the same area, and it was headed toward Red Lake. So we headed up there after it; snow was deep, and we had no snowshoes, so our going was rough. We finally got up to the bear's tracks and followed them. The tracks looked like the bear was going to go on over the pass to Red Lake. But the bear *spotted* us when we got up on an open ridge. Well, this bear *also* circled and came back for us. When it got right across the creek from us on a big boulder, the bear stood up on it's hind legs for a better look at us. That's when the next hunter shot — he was also using silvertip bullets — and he had to shoot nine times to kill that bear, too.

"Bears often try to sneak around on you to get your scent if they spot you first. So far though, I've never had a bear sneak up from the rear and charge. I guess if any sneaked up on me that I failed to see, they ran away as soon as they got my scent.''

Noise is another important element to consider for successful Brown Bear hunting. Clumsy hunters don't score, because silence is the name of the game.

"When you get close to a bear,'' says Talifson, "you can't be too careful about noise from dry grass, weeds, sticks, and brush. Your clothes and boots will rub on the brush, and if you don't watch your step, you'll break some stick or something, and alarm the bear to your presence. Trouble is, sometimes when going through brush you can't see the bear, but it will hear you coming, then spot you, and sneak around to get your wind.''

Noise can also be a great detriment in the spring, when crusty snow covers the ground. Talifson learned this lesson early in his career also.

''We spotted a bear high up on the hill, amid alders and brush, and in pretty deep snow, ''he recalls. ''We got up above the bear, and my hunter wasn't impressed with its size. So he asked me, as quite a few hunters do, to go down and measure the bear's tracks in the snow, to see how big it was. Well, I had to get pretty close to the bear to get at its tracks; but when I went back to the hunter, the bear heard me going through the crusty snow.''

''The bear stood up, and the hunter shot it, but not mortally; he hit it in the throat. Well, down the hill that bear came, towards me, then past me, and finally out into the valley below. We had to track the bear quite a ways before we got it.''

Regardless of the season, noise is a troublesome factor for any bear hunter to contend with. Hunters can avoid many pitfalls by wearing wool outer garments because they tend to make less noise in brush than other types of cloth. Avoid nylon or similar materials. Those often are the noisiest. Wear raingear only when it's raining, because these tend to be noisy, too. Silence always is essential to success.

Besides the bear's senses of smell, sight and hearing, the hunter's own sense of sight is perhaps the biggest single factor that he must contend with. Basically, the hunter needs to utilize his ability to see to it's fullest potential. The grass and leaves fought to maintain silence may also be his greatest impediment to good vision. Talifson explains why.

''You can't spot a bear very easily when the grass is chest high on a man,'' he says, ''and if a lot of leaves are still on the alders, bears can be lying in them and never be seen. As a prime example, I had one hunter that I put up on a big bear: it was in dense willows just ten feet away, but we couldn't see it until it stood up. The hunter shot it, and as it came down off of it's hind feet, I though we'd had it for sure. But fortunately, the animal turned and ran. We finally killed the bear, but I'll never forget how close we came to getting mauled.''

"A lot of times you'll spot bears from up high. You're up on a hill glassing, and the animal is out in the valley in flats covered with alders and willows. Then when you get down to it's level, you can't see the bear because of all of the brush. Often the bear gets away in those situations."

"Snow is another thing that affects your sight when hunting. In the fall, a little snow is a good thing because it makes it easy to see where bears have been, and to spot them once you've caught up.

"Conversely, in the spring, when bears aren't moving about to any great extent, a light snow can hurt your hunting. A bear might lie in one spot for days. But if you can spot it's tracks with your binoculars, you sometimes can simply follow the tracks by sight and find the animal's location. But if a fresh snow covers those tracks, you won't know where to look. You may see the bear lying up there, but mistake it for a rock because it doesn't move.

"Usually, in a snowy spring, you spend a lot of time glassing every dark object in sight. You don't want to overlook anything that could possibly be a bear. A lot of times a bear will lay outside it's den for days without moving. When the bear does move, it may only move it's paw — and then only slightly. If you are fortunate enough to spot the motion, then you've found a bear.

"We've sat and watched 'rocks' for days, and we've even had our hunters and packers laugh at us for doing it. But they stop laughing when the 'rock' turns over and stands up. Sometimes the bear will be lying on it's back — belly up — with it's legs extended vertically so that it's paws look like 'eagles'. There's no end to the appearances of bears at first glimpse in the spring. Consequently, we've wound up actually stalking rocks that were mistaken for bears.

"I had some hunters out and we'd looked for a long while at what appeared to be two big bears. But when we got up to them, they turned out to be big rocks covered with moss. The moss had looked just like fur blowing in the breeze because shadows from moving branches were waving back and forth across the rocks."

After hunters and guides have managed to stalk their game within shooting range, the rather important question of bullet placement becomes paramount. When dealing with a huge beast such as the Kodiak Brown Bear, this issue is critical. P & T have several views on this topic, too.

"I've had hunters shoot bears in just about every spot on the animals' bodies," says Talifson. "If the hunter hits the bear in the throat or jaw, the animal will be terribly injured and just as dangerous. It may go miles and miles without stopping.

"One hunter I remember shot his bear in the neck while it was asleep. The one shot was solid and the only bear movement I detected afterwards was slight relaxation of its leg. I prefer a neck shot. But it's hard to make. You just have to make a mental picture of that bone and squeeze the trigger. Many times you wind up cutting the windpipe. But if you hit the bone, a Brown Bear will go right down. Neck shots aren't always so successful though, and sho·:ld only be attempted by good marksmen who are very familiar with the bear's anatomy.

"As a rule, a hunter should try to completely disable the bear with his first shot. This means hitting the animal in its shoulder to knock it off of its feet. Then, with the bear crippled, the hunter can continue shooting until it's dead — and stops moving.

"Very few bears die with one shot. Four to six shots better represents the average. The animals are just too big and too powerful to be killed with single shots consistently. Some bears can take a dozen shots without dying. This is why we don't encourage hunters to shoot rifles smaller than the .300 magnum.

"When a bear is wounded, but fails to go down, it often bolts for brush. When this happens, everyone who can safely do so, ought to fire at it to keep it from getting into cover.

"A hunter, two assistants, and I were hunting at Karluk Lake one year, and the hunter had been put up on a large bear by my two assistants. I was watching their progress from some distance. After the hunter shot, I heard a 'whump' and the bear began running back and forth in front of the men. Then my two assistants began shooting, too, and I heard several more 'whumps,' but the animal still didn't go down. Finally, the bear headed for brush.

"I figured that the bear was badly hurt. I was standing alone, quite a ways off. I had my rifle slung over my shoulder while I watched with binoculars. When the bear started for brush, I simply unslung my rifle, fired one shot, watched the bear go down, and quickly reslung my rifle. Upon examination of the bear, however, there was only one hole in it, and my .375 had made it. The hunter never realized what had happened.

"Sometimes you can't be certain whether a bear is getting hit; but if it may have been hit, and it heads for brush, you've got a duty to act decisively.

"Some bears don't flinch when hit. I had a hunter up Red River, and he shot the bear from behind while it was lying down. The bear jumped up, but just stood there looking in the opposite direction. The bear had taken this shot low — up the rib cage. The hunter's second shot sliced fat across the bear's back, rendering a long strip of oil as it cut. Finally, the hunter shot the bear right in the anus — a bullseye — and the animal collapsed instantly. The last bullet went up into the heart and lungs.

"Another consideration in bullet placement is possible damage to trophy skulls when head shots are attempted. The bear taken by my hunter, Dave Connor, might have been Brown Bear number one in the Boone and Crockett Record Book if it hadn't been hit in the head. The skull lost an inch or better at its rear base where the bullet knocked out a big chuck of bone. Because of the missing bone, the skull only ranked number thirteen."

The elder guides of Olga bay have every reason to feel confident about their accumulated knowledge of Brown Bear hunting.

"But," adds Pinnell, "we'll never learn it all."

The afternoon faded as our conversation waned. Talifson lit his pipe while Pinnell busied himself with letters — letters from hunters who dreamed of hunting the big bear. My stint on Kodiak was ending. I had packed many miles through the heart of Brown Bear territory in search of bears and more knowledge about their habits and habitat. I had enjoyed a lengthy visit with P & T, who probably know more about bruins than any two bear men alive. I was thankful, because I had been able to find, and follow, the track of the Kodiak.